The Seasons of Your Career

How to Master the Cycles of Career Change

Kathy Sanborn with Wayne R. Ricci

Contemporary Books

Chicago   New York   San Francisco   Lisbon   London   Madrid   Mexico City
Milan   New Delhi   San Juan   Seoul   Singapore   Sydney   Toronto

Library of Congress Cataloging-in-Publication Data

Sanborn , Kathy.
    The seasons of your career : how to master the cycles of career change / Kathy
    Sanborn with Wayne R. Ricci.
        p.   cm.
    ISBN 0-07-140608-5
    1. Career changes.   I. Ricci, Wayne R.   II. Title.

HF5384.S26   2003
650.14—dc21   2002034971

We dedicate this book to our parents,
Dolores and Charles, Thelma and Richard,
and to our daughters, Cherie, Alicia, and Meilani.

1 2 3 4 5 6 7 8 9 0   AGM/AGM   2 1 0 9 8 7 6 5 4 3

ISBN 0-07-140608-5

McGraw-Hill books are available at special quantity discounts to use as premiums and sales
promotions, or for use in corporate training programs. For more information, please write to
the Director of Special Sales, Professional Publishing, McGraw-Hill, Two Penn Plaza, New
York, NY 10121-2298. Or contact your local bookstore.

This book is printed on acid-free paper.

CONTENTS

PREFACE

Live each season as it passes; breathe the air, drink the drink,
taste the fruit, and resign yourself to the influences of each.
—HENRY DAVID THOREAU

WHETHER ONE IS twenty years old and in her first job or fifty-five and contemplating a job change, there are specific seasons to every person's career. In this book, we'll teach you how to recognize the seasons of your career and show you how to master the career cycles that you'll encounter throughout your working life. Knowledge is power—once you have a solid understanding of your own career season, you will be able to glide through the cycles of change with confidence. Keep reading, and discover how you can use this book as your tool for lifelong job fulfillment.

Due to a combination of job market volatility and greater motivation to find satisfying work, people are changing career paths more frequently than ever before. This has resulted in younger workers replacing an unrewarding vocation with one that is better suited to their interests, talents, and dreams. Older workers are beginning fresh jobs at what would have been considered retirement age less than a generation ago. All in all, career fulfillment is becoming a necessary ingredient of our lives.

This book is dedicated to providing you ways to master the cycles of career change as well as to find an ideal path of service. Because you may spend at least a third of your life at work, you must consider carefully what your life's occupation should be. Working in a profession that doesn't fulfill you will affect every other area of your life. In fact, you have within you a specific career path of service that suits you to a tee. In these pages, we'll help you to discover that path.

Perhaps you had childhood ideas of what you would like to do for a living as an adult. Some of us kept our youthful dreams alive, while others put them aside for a later day. Still others let their career dreams become nightmares; they're stuck in work they've grown to resent—with no apparent way out.

A few months ago, Bill began to notice the stirrings of discontent as he went through his day as an elementary schoolteacher. At first, he had enjoyed the idea of training young minds, but the seemingly endless staff meetings, paperwork, and committee assignments had left him increasingly frustrated. Today Bill has a hard time getting up in the morning because he dreads going to work at the school.

Carla is a single parent and busy professional marketing executive. Ambitious and hardworking, she is a leading light in her organization, and has received kudos for her innovative projects and dedication to her employer's mission and values. Every hour of Carla's day is tightly scheduled, which leaves her very little time for herself or her family. Because Carla appreciates her comfortable, upscale way of living, she spends twelve hours a day on the job. Lately, though, she's been feeling the strain of her commitment to her career, and she's questioning her ability to balance work demands and family life.

Bill and Carla are not alone. Research tells us that many people work in jobs they don't enjoy. Maybe you've said things like, "I wish it were Friday," or, "The weekend was too short!" Maybe you're that busy executive who keeps complaining that you don't have enough time for yourself or your family because you're working so hard. It doesn't have to be that way.

Because your workplace is where you spend most of your waking hours, why should you pass your time doing a job that doesn't fulfill your dreams? By putting into practice the guidelines presented in this book, you will begin a journey of increased personal growth and career fulfillment. Throughout these pages, we'll be pointing out ways you can make the very best of whichever career season you're in. We'll offer you helpful tips, inspiring stories, and useful tools along the way. Whether you are just starting out in the workforce or have been climbing the career ladder for quite some time, you will gain valuable information by using this book.

Drawn from our own professional experience in a busy consulting practice, *The Seasons of Your Career* will be your guide to achieving the ultimate in career success—providing heartfelt service to others while fulfilling your own career dreams. Stick with us, and we'll guide you down the path of career success!

ACKNOWLEDGMENTS

WE WOULD LIKE TO give special thanks to the many clients and others whose stories are included in this book. (For purposes of contributor confidentiality, all names in the stories have been changed.) We are indebted to Maggie Burton, Grace Keller, Paul Pittana, and Nuria Duran for their comments as well.

Our warmest appreciation goes out to Jessica Lichtenstein and Joëlle Delbourgo, without whom this book would not have been written. To Denise Betts, our editor at Contemporary Books, goes our profound gratitude for believing that we had something worthwhile to say, and for being a sheer joy to work with.

TO EVERYTHING
THERE IS A SEASON

To be interested in the changing seasons is a happier state of mind than to be hopelessly in love with spring.
—GEORGE SANTAYANA

THE SEASONS OF YOUR CAREER are based on the seasons of nature: Spring, Summer, Autumn, and Winter. Whether it's once or many times per lifetime, each of us goes through the career season cycle. From the fresh opportunities represented by Spring, to the end of the career cycle designated by Winter, the cycle of the seasons goes by in a unique way for each individual.

In the ideal manifestation of the career season cycle, each return to Spring marks a new, higher level, an upward spiral of learning and achievement. Eventually, through the process of the seasons, you will discover the most fertile ground in which to share your talents with the world. When you find the right path of service, it will reward you. It will also benefit everyone else you come into contact with as you perform your work because your career becomes a joy.

There are no set time frames for the changeover between seasons. You could transition from Spring to Summer in one month and then go from Summer to Autumn in seven years. It is very possible to be in a Summer phase, for example, and go rather rapidly to a Winter one, as in the case of termination, layoff, or other personal crisis. Because of factors such as your thoughts, feelings, and life events, the timing of your career seasons cannot be charted with precision.

Like the sequence of birth through death, there will be peaks and valleys throughout your career journey. In certain cases, you could transition swiftly from Spring to Winter. If you take a shortcut to success by using ill-advised or even dishonest means, you could bypass your natural Summer season of achievement and go straight to an unanticipated Winter.

There are distinct signposts to each season, though not every person will experience all seasons in the same manner. For instance, some winters in nature can vary according to the environment, with some areas being wetter than others, stormier than others, and so on. Individual differences notwithstanding, your own Winter career season will not be able to masquerade as another season. It will be quite discernible as your very own Winter.

Your path of service will involve finding an exact fit in a career that you love and, through that placement, using your special talents to make a positive impact on the world. By seeking out and finding a specific career niche that brings you joy, you will be in a position to enhance society. You'll be adding to the happiness of the people you serve by performing your work with enthusiasm and competence, you'll be spreading good cheer to the people in your inner circle, and you'll have the enormous satisfaction of doing something worthwhile. In this book, you'll discover how to find your own career path of service.

First we'll give you the methods to determine which career season you're currently experiencing and how to make the most of it. By establishing which career season you're in, you will be taking the first step toward understanding your professional path within the framework of the changing flow of seasons.

Throughout these pages, we'll be sharing the information you need regarding achieving career fulfillment in any season. Let's begin by discussing some basic characteristics of Spring, Summer, Autumn, and Winter. Later on in the book, you'll learn about the four career seasons in detail.

SPRING

Spring is the season when the seeds are planted to produce new growth, and if you're in the Spring season of your career, you're busy laying the groundwork for job success to come. You may be doing research on a new career field, or starting a business venture. You could be experiencing renewed excitement for the career you've been involved in all along. Anything appears possible at this stage of the game—there's nowhere to go but up. The way to recognize the Spring career season is by its seeds of new beginnings.

As a Spring individual, you might have decided to seek fresh employment avenues, and doors may now open to new opportunities. The Spring career season offers opportunity and challenge. You have the opportunities fanning out before you in all directions. Your challenge is to select the right career path and to show that you are up to the task of learning your new job.

The ideal way to handle the Spring season is to be a person of energy, with a positive attitude and assertive behavior. Changing your mental outlook to a more affirmative one will help you to achieve your Spring goals.

Remember we said we'd be giving you tips on how to make the best of every career season? This is your first one:

> *If you are in the Spring season of your career, it is crucial that you remain positive and optimistic. Spring is the time for energy and enthusiasm, and to plant the seeds of opportunity you'll first want to make sure your mental state is a constructive one. If you need some help keeping upbeat, jump ahead and read Chapter 5, "The Fifteen Rules for Staying Positive."*

SUMMER

We can identify the Summer career season by its aura of competence and achievement. As an individual in the Summer season, you may have reached the pinnacle of your career, or may be on the verge of doing so. Here, in Summer, you're maintaining your initial enthusiasm for your job, and likely reaping the harvest of your ambitions. The season of Summer is a time of enjoying the fruits of Spring's labors.

You, the Summer worker, are successfully using your talents to enhance your career ambitions. During the stages of Summer, you may be experiencing a slow rise in your job or meteoric one, depending on your individual circumstances. Having carefully planted the seeds of success while in the Spring phase, you can now reap your rewards. Here's a hot tip for you, the Summer individual.

> *It is paramount for you, as a Summer person, to keep your ego in check as you ride the wave of career fulfillment. Whether you are nineteen or fifty, job success can be a heady thing. Danger signs of an out-of-control ego are: showing little consideration for other people; feeling superior to others; needing to associate*

with only the "right" people; and desiring the attentions and compliments of others in order to feel secure within yourself. If you feel your ego needs to be managed, head for Chapter 2, "Career Master Thinking."

AUTUMN

Treading water is the key phrase associated with the Autumn career season. This season gives you the opportunity to assess the job fulfillment you've achieved thus far, and to decide whether to take action in another direction, or to remain in your cozy niche for the duration of your career. As an Autumn person, the choice is yours.

You can be at a crossroads in your employment life in the Autumn career season. Perhaps in a job that once showed promise but has since changed, you may find yourself bored, yet comfortable, with the steady paycheck and lack of challenge your position provides.

Autumn can be a time of relative career inactivity when achievement is not a driving force. You may have no particular reason to upset the applecart. With no identifiable job goals to pursue, you swim the employment seas with little forward motion. Your motivation for growth may be missing in the Autumn phase. You may remain in a job that you don't really desire.

Based on your assessment of your level of career fulfillment, and on whether you wish to take action for change, Autumn can be a time of stagnation or renewal. There is no one correct choice—you must decide the best course for yourself. If job fulfillment is important to you, take heed—and take action.

If you are in the Autumn phase of your career cycle, it's important for you to listen to your heart as to what you need to do next on your professional path. Do you stay where you are, in the comfort zone, or do you add exhilaration to your life by striking out into uncharted employment territory? To help you decide, read Chapter 8, "Autumn: The Season of Changing Colors."

WINTER

The Winter season is the end of a career or job cycle. If you are experiencing this season, you may find yourself at a crisis point, where circumstances could arise that might be completely outside of your control, such as layoff or business closure. Yet Winter doesn't have to be a time of crisis at all; it can serve as a marker of completion for a career life that has gone by. Perhaps you have come to realize that your current career holds no future or fulfillment. In this case, you must take the time to assess your current position, how and when you want to close this chapter of your career, and how you will move forward into the Spring of your next career or position. In any event, you have reached the end of a particular career cycle, and now find that a new door of opportunity is opening, even as the old door is closing after you.

The Winter season is a period of preparation and patience which, if carefully managed, can set the stage for successful Spring beginnings. After all, everyone must experience Winter at some point— it is a natural part of the cycle and an important part of growth on a personal or professional level. You can make more progress toward self-awareness during Winter than in any other season because there's no looking back—the old door is closing behind you.

A drastic change in the status quo is the key to understanding the Winter season. Now you are experiencing a phase of challenge + opportunity. Out of every challenge comes the seed of a fresh beginning. Taking action on the signs of new opportunity instead of letting them pass you by will propel you into the next season of Spring.

Going through the Winter season is a little like getting an immunization shot in the doctor's office—it can be painful at

the time, but its ultimate value far outweighs the temporary dis-
comfort. As a Winter individual, you are likely to undergo an
enormous career transformation, no matter what factors
prompted you to do so. Whether it was your own choice or
another's decision, you are on a new road. For inspiring words
about how to master your own personal Winter, see Chapter 9,
"Winter: A Journey Through the Snowy Season."

WHAT'S YOUR SEASON?

Once you discover your current position in the cycle of seasons, you'll be able to handle your own professional path more easily. Having the knowledge about your career season cycles will benefit you throughout your professional life by helping you to adjust comfortably to job transitions and employment surprises. Moreover, becoming familiar with the career seasons will aid you in planning for ultimate job success and complete career fulfillment. Take the following quiz to determine your own career season.

WHAT SEASON AM I IN?

Check an answer to each question to find out your career season. There are no right or wrong answers.

	Agree	Disagree
1. I've started a job in the last six months.	___	___
2. I find myself daydreaming about new jobs from time to time.	___	___
✘ 3. I am not working toward any new goals.	___	___
4. Even if they didn't pay me, if I could afford it, I'd work here!	___	___

	Agree	Disagree
5. I've achieved most of the goals I've set for myself in this job.	____	____
6. It's too late for me to try another career.	____	____
7. My job skills need to be updated or improved a great deal.	____	____
✓ 8. My job doesn't challenge me the way it used to.	____	____
9. I've received a raise for my excellent job performance.	____	____
10. A friend or relative told me I needed to work in this career because it's a secure job.	____	____
11. I'm tired all the time.	____	____
12. I get a lot of praise from my boss and coworkers.	____	____
13. I look forward to going to work each day.	____	____
✓ 14. I've been feeling bored at work for a long time.	____	____
15. I've been out of the workforce for years now.	____	____
16. No goal is too hard for me to achieve.	____	____
17. What's a promotion? As long as I've been here, I've never seen one!	____	____
18. I want to learn all I can about this job.	____	____

	Agree	Disagree
19. I get great satisfaction from my job.	_____	_____
20. I just graduated from school and I'm ready to find the right job.	_____	_____

KEY TO YOUR CAREER SEASON

On the key below, score a point for each season that matches a check mark on the Agree column of your answer sheet. (You'll notice that there are two seasons listed for some of the questions in the scoring key below—give yourself one point for each of those seasons.) Enter your totals in the chart below.

1. Spring

2. Autumn

♪ 3. Autumn

4. Summer

5. Summer, Autumn

6. Autumn, Winter

7. Spring, Winter

✔ 8. Autumn, Winter

9. Summer

10. Autumn

11. Autumn, Winter

12. Summer

13. Spring, Summer

✔ 14. Autumn, Winter

15. Spring, Winter

16. Spring, Summer

17. Autumn, Winter

18. Spring

19. Summer

20. Spring

My Totals

Spring	Summer	Autumn	Winter
_____	_____	_____	_____

Your career season is the one with the most points. If you have a tie, you may be in a situation that has elements of two or more seasons. If so, study the season descriptions carefully to determine which season fits you best.

My career season is _____.

Now you know which career season applies to you at this point on your employment path. Whether Spring, Summer, Autumn, or Winter, your particular season can be a positive and a productive one. Every season has important characteristics and typical patterns with something valuable to offer.

AGE THROUGH THE SEASONS

Individuals of every age can experience any of the career seasons. A septuagenarian can be in the Spring of his career, while a woman in her early twenties may find herself in Winter.

A professional woman of fifty in her Autumn career season was considering returning to school to obtain her doctorate in psychology, but she had deep concerns about attempting to achieve such a goal at her age. Lunching one day with a friend, she raised the subject of her career dilemma, mentioning that she'd be about fifty-five by the time she got her Ph.D. The friend responded with a smile, "How old would you be anyway?" She went on to get her degree.

When you hold expectations about the kinds of positions you are likely to find at a certain age, it can create barriers to making positive career changes. Considering certain activities or jobs age-appropriate can lead you to exclude the very work that suits you best. After all, you don't want to miss a great opportunity because you feel you are too old or not experienced enough.

While there are mature workers in any career season, it would be an oversight to say that older individuals should throw caution to the wind when considering a career change. Many older people may view retirement as a transition point, where they can reawaken an earlier career dream once abandoned, or choose a brand-new field altogether.

However, a seventy-year-old may not wish to begin a new career life in Spring. Indeed, it may not even be in her best interest to do so. She may be dealing with health issues or other considerations that could prevent her from considering new employment. Electing to remain retired can be a viable and rewarding choice for any mature person.

Because mature workers have to consider how long they wish to remain working, they should weigh many factors before taking the plunge to a new career. Some older workers feel that by continuing to work they'll be provided with mental stimulation, productive activity, and social interaction—all vital to happiness and well-being. For those individuals, making a career transition could be a way of keeping enthusiasm high. On the other hand, for mature individuals who've opted for relaxing days in retirement, a career change wouldn't even be an issue.

Very young career seekers may experience the catch-22 of not having enough experience to get a job in their ideal field, but being denied the job that would provide the required experience. If they are not persistent in the quest to break into an exciting career, they may choose to quit before the ideal job opportunity arises.

A young adult may need time to mature into a worker with a calling. Depending on the person, a dream career may not materialize until midlife or even later. This can be due to factors such as fear, being out of touch with one's inner wisdom, and doubt about one's abilities to do the job that calls one's name. There will be those in their twenties or even younger whose stars will rise early because they are in tune with their career dreams, while other youthful workers will have their own dates with career destiny much later.

STORIES OF THE SEASONS

Remember Bill and Carla, the two people we introduced in the very beginning of this book? Bill was the elementary schoolteacher, growing increasingly restless with the administrative demands of his job, and thus experiencing a lack of enthusiasm for his teaching position. He had just crossed over into the Autumn season—at one time he had been excited about his job, but things had definitely changed. What could Bill do to renew his flagging interest in his chosen profession? Or did Bill need to look in another career direction entirely?

By doing a thorough self-assessment and following the goal achievement techniques discussed later in the book, Bill discovered that he had an interest in working as a staff development trainer for a private company, and he began to explore that possibility while remaining in his teaching position. He realized that it was the role of instructor that he had relished most, and he knew he could transfer his teaching skills to a variety of other settings. Now Bill is happily working at his new position, which requires much less paperwork, and he is able to devote his full energies to his love of teaching. Did he give up on training young minds? No; Bill is an active volunteer mentor to disadvantaged children. Now Bill is in the Spring season of his career, with a new start and a world of possibilities ahead of him.

Bill experienced a brief Winter season as he prepared to leave his old job. As soon as he became aware of his career needs in the Autumn season, Bill took quick action to make the necessary job changes. Had Bill decided to ignore his discontent instead of addressing his concerns, he could have remained indefinitely in the career limbo of Autumn. By choosing to move easily through Winter, Bill handled his cycle of seasons in the best possible way.

Carla, the divorced marketing executive with a twelve-hour workday, had two young children and a house right out of *Better Homes and Gardens*. Because she had acquired a reputation for excellence on the job, Carla was on a fast track to success. Recently, Carla had begun to feel the pressure of the combination of her long work hours and the lack of private time for herself and her children. Carla had been feeling exhausted and overwhelmed, with few moments to relax and unwind during the day. Once thriving on the challenge of her fast-paced job, Carla realized that she needed to reevaluate her priorities at this point in her life. The late Summer season of her career was the perfect time for Carla to take stock of her options and make the appropriate adjustments.

Because Carla still enjoyed her work, the troubling issue for her was not career change, but the need for balancing her job with her children's frequent requests to spend quality time with her. How could she improve her late Summer situation and achieve overall balance in her life?

After completing some of the worksheets and quizzes you'll be using in this book, Carla had a better understanding of her own need for achievement and learned how to make important modifications in her definition of success to provide more quality time for herself and her children. Carla then took action to accomplish her objective by decreasing the amount of time she spent at the office. After reaching an agreement with her employer, Carla chose to telecommute for a portion of each workday. Still in the Summer season of her career, Carla finally has balanced her rewarding career with her family life.

Already you've gotten your feet wet by seeing how the career seasons operate in the lives of working people like you. By using the techniques in this book, you'll be able to make positive career changes.

In this chapter you've learned about the career season cycle and discovered which of the seasons matches your current career path. In the following chapters, we give you the information you need to sail through the cycles of the seasons with confidence. The more you understand the flow of the career seasons, the better you will be able to correct your course with the changing conditions, and to make those adjustments at the right time. Now you're ready to go on to the next chapter, "Career Master Thinking," in which you'll learn how to transform your thoughts into powerful tools that will be valuable for success in any career season.

2

CAREER MASTER THINKING

All the resources we need are in the mind.
—THEODORE ROOSEVELT

LIFE IS TOO SHORT to waste time doing something that doesn't bring you joy or fulfillment. The famed humanistic psychologist Abraham Maslow theorized that very few people achieve self-actualization, which, simply stated, means not many of us become all that we can be. Are *you* utilizing your skills and talents to become all that you can be?

The first step to fulfilling your potential is to learn to choose your thoughts wisely and to allow only positive thoughts into your consciousness. This will help you master your critical-thinking skills and enable you to sail gracefully through any career state. By focusing on your mind and how it works, you will be able to (1) create a career dream that you can really achieve, (2) control your negative thoughts and promote positive ones, (3) put in motion a career plan that will really work, and (4) apply these principles successfully no matter which career season you're in.

In many ways, your mind is like fertile soil: You plant the seeds (thoughts) and your mind generates flora (results). By taking care to plant only positive and constructive thoughts, you'll achieve the results you're looking for.

In the Spring season, for example, you plant seeds of new beginnings. In the Summer you plant seeds of achievement. Seeds of renewal can be planted in Autumn, and Winter's plantings will likely be seeds of preparation.

An unproductive way to plant your thoughts is to succumb to inner beliefs such as (1) "I'm not smart enough to get the job I really want"; (2) "It would take forever to get the degree I need"; (3) "I'm too old to start over"; (4) "There are too many obstacles in my way"—and the list goes on!

The right way to seed the soil of your mind is by dropping in positive inner statements such as (1) "It's what I really want to do, so it's worth the time and energy it takes to get it"; (2) "Anything worthwhile takes effort"; (3) "I deserve the career I want"; and (4) "I have all the talent I need to succeed in my chosen career."

If properly trained and used, your mind is a marvelous tool. It acts on the information you feed it. If negative (destructive) thoughts consistently flow through your mind, you will be better served by changing the way you allow your mind to operate.

IF THE THOUGHT ISN'T POSITIVE, GET RID OF IT!

Positive, or constructive, thoughts are the only ones you'll want to use to achieve your goals. Get rid of critical and unkind thoughts about yourself or others—thoughts of doubt, failure, or fear, and worries about all the thousands of possible disasters that could happen to you. Whatever you focus on expands—the more positive thoughts you create, the more favorable results you'll see. The same holds true for negative thoughts.

Without proper monitoring, our minds will generate all kinds of thoughts, many of which we can do without. Be conscious of your thoughts and patterns of thinking. When you catch yourself in a negative thought, say to yourself, "I accept only positive thoughts in my life." At first you may have to repeat that phrase over and over because your mind may be in the habit of generating a lot of negativity. After practice, however, you'll find that you've been successful in retraining yourself to think like the winners of the world.

The goal of replacing your pessimistic thoughts with upbeat ones is to teach your mind to maintain a positive attitude in any event. With time and practice you'll become adept at reorganizing your thought patterns and you'll notice that your days are happier as a result of this training.

Once you learn how to monitor your thoughts and how to change them from negative to positive, the work doesn't stop there. You will need to practice these skills for the rest of your life—think of them as exercise for your mind. Just as it is more beneficial to do physical exercise on a regular basis, your mental techniques are most helpful when practiced consistently.

Sometimes it's not easy to concentrate only on constructive thoughts. When circumstances are pleasant, it's far easier to think in a positive way. When you're faced with life's challenges, it can take a little more effort on your part to maintain a cheerful mental outlook.

The only limits you have are the ones in your own mind. Of course, being human, you'll have some moments when it takes monumental effort to stay upbeat, especially if you're exceptionally tired from overwork or stressed due to life's many challenges.

THE SPRING MASTER THINKER

Because you're embracing new opportunities in Spring, you could be experiencing some feelings of doubt or uncertainty at this point. Perhaps you question whether you can succeed in your new position, or you feel a little over your head in your chosen field. Maybe you've come from a job with a lot of responsibility and status to one where you will have to prove yourself all over again.

To make the best of your Spring season, you can use career master thinking principles to assuage any concerns you might have about acclimating to new work. Worrying about your ability to succeed in your career will hold you back from growing and contributing on the job, so your first order of business is to focus on the strengths and skills that got you the position in the first place. With determination and targeted action, you'll rise to the occasion and continue to build confidence in your capability to realize your goals.

Barbara, a forty-one-year-old former cop, is making a career move to instructing high school students. Her spirits are high and her skills are top-notch, so the odds are great that she'll be able to transition easily to her new post. Barbara learned to manage her thoughts and to get rid of any that weren't helping her to reach her goals. As a result of her experiences as a police officer, she used to worry excessively about the people she loved—whether they were healthy, safe, and happy. These thoughts of deep concern about others were getting in the way of her peace of mind, and until she banished them they got in the way of her ability to make a successful career transition. Now that she's able to put her full attention on her new teaching career, Barbara is able to benefit from her Spring career season. Just as Barbara did, you can learn to control any thoughts that detract from your contentment and serenity.

Your thoughts, whether positive or negative, determine the quality of life that you experience. Some people go through serious illness or other extreme difficulties with a smile and good cheer. How do they do it? Rather than dwell on their troubles, they focus on their blessings. As a Spring individual, you should welcome the new opportunities and possibilities ahead of you without negatively focusing on an uncertain future.

THOUGHTS OF SUMMER SUCCESS

You're in the season of climbing to the top, and practicing career master thinking can help you reach your peak of achievement. In Summer you might be feeling discouraged because your goal could be taking longer than you'd planned. Perhaps you're too attached to a particular career outcome or fearful that others are gaining on you in the race for promotion. You might be worried about the possibility that you'll become outmoded, and thus discarded, at work. By playing the career achievement game all day long, you may find yourself unable to relax or to enjoy any private time outside of work. You can overcome any of those negative ways of thinking by using the practical tools in this chapter. With thought management and prudent action, your Summer season can be one of enormous fulfillment.

Betty, a talented graphic designer, had been working quite successfully for someone else until three years ago when she decided to launch her own design business. A positive thinker by nature, Betty has made a lifelong habit of using spiritual principles to guide her on her career path. Techniques of nonattachment and meditation have helped Betty to stay upbeat and focused while she concentrates on building her business. She continues to build her clientele and to provide her services with enthusiasm. Betty's Summer season is flowing smoothly, thanks to her high level of career master thinking.

MASTER THINKING IN AUTUMN

In the Autumn phase, career master thinking is crucial if you want to shake off the work doldrums. You may have built a habit of negative or pessimistic thinking that is holding you back from further growth or achievement. Comfortable in a post of little challenge, you may be biding your time until layoff or retirement. Part of your task in Autumn is to take stock of your thoughts and make any necessary changes. Even though you have the desire to break out of a rut, you might feel unable to take a step toward career growth. You may have thoughts that you're not as talented as other people, and these thoughts may be keeping you from attempting the bigger career dreams you've got tucked away in your mind.

Gloria has been working as a retail store manager for fifteen years. The wages are relatively low, and long hours on her feet have taken their toll. Although bright and vivacious, Gloria feels that she lacks enough education to break out of a job that, more and more, appears to be a career dead end. Though she is still young, Gloria is nonetheless beginning to feel that it's too late for change. She grins and bears it through each workday wondering if she will ever get up the courage to try something new. Gloria is a prime candidate for the principles of career master thinking. Her belief that she can't get out of her career dilemma will be a reality unless she takes steps to rewrite those beliefs.

If you find yourself with professional dreams that are not being fulfilled, you will want to adjust your own thinking and behavior. Thoughts of doubt or fear can be extremely problematic for anyone who desires job success. Most of the time, negative beliefs have little basis in fact, and serve only to prevent you from going after your true ambitions. Thoughts of doubt, fear, or worry are like weeds in a beautiful garden. You can pull them out and make your garden a delight once again.

THE WINTER WONDERER

The Winter season can be a time of preparation after termination or retirement. You may begin to realize that you are meant to do more than while away the hours in a stagnant job. It's really a period of new opportunity, a time to initiate a successful voluntary or involuntary career transition. It's easy to fall into a negative thinking pattern when this kind of change takes place. That's why career master thinking is so important in the Winter season.

If you've lost your job, you might be feeling as if the bottom's dropped out of your world. Instead of focusing on your unique talents and years of valuable work experience in order to move ahead to the next career opportunity, maybe you're bemoaning your situation. Perhaps you feel you're too old for a fresh start; you have doubts about whether you'll have sufficient energy to meet the next set of challenges or whether you are qualified for your ideal career. You may question whether you have the time and money to pursue additional training and education. Just remember that with careful planning and action, you'll be able to leap over any career hurdles.

Joyce was recently laid off from her job in the airline industry. As a flight attendant, she had found a way to work and travel the world at the same time. Now she's searching the want ads and registering with employment agencies. Her attitude is positive, and she realizes that being laid off can happen to anyone. Joyce spends little time brooding about what she can't change. She trusts that the right job will come along. Her optimistic viewpoint will help keep her spirits high as she enthusiastically and tirelessly navigates the Winter of her career.

MASTER THINKING QUIZ

Now let's take a quiz to see how you rate as a career master thinker. Then you'll learn about concepts that will help you improve your mindset. On the line next to each statement, write T (True) if the statement applies to you and F (False) if it does not.

Master Thinking Quiz

1. I'm a positive person most of the time. _____

2. I sometimes question whether I'm as talented as other people. _____

3. Too often I'm moody and irritable. _____

4. I can accomplish anything I set my mind to. _____

5. Nothing ever happens for me, no matter what I do. _____

6. Usually, I listen to my family and friends before I make career decisions. _____

7. I usually don't gossip or find fault with others. _____

8. Right now, my job doesn't offer me much, but I'm staying anyway. _____

9. At work, I find plenty to complain about. _____

10. I have confidence that I will achieve my goals. _____

11. Setbacks are only positive learning experiences for me. _____

12. I guess I just don't have it in me to reach my career dreams. _____

13. My work and personal relationships are caring and genuine. _____

14. I've always been able to enjoy any job I've had. _____

15. I just sort of fell into my career. _____

Your Career Master Thinking Score

Add the total points for your answers and read the key to determine your master thinking score.

Question	True	False	Points
1.	2 points	1 point	_____
2.	1 point	2 points	_____
3.	1 point	2 points	_____
4.	2 points	1 point	_____
5.	1 point	2 points	_____
6.	1 point	2 points	_____
7.	2 points	1 point	_____
8.	1 point	2 points	_____
9.	1 point	2 points	_____
10.	2 points	1 point	_____
11.	2 points	1 point	_____
12.	1 point	2 points	_____
13.	2 points	1 point	_____
14.	2 points	1 point	_____
15.	1 point	2 points	_____

GRAND TOTAL: _____

If you scored between 26 and 30 points, congratulations—you're an expert master thinker!

If you scored between 20 and 25 points, you may want to work on your career master thinking skills a bit more.

If you scored 19 or below, you need a major overhaul in career master thinking.

If your score indicates that you have some work to do on your career master thinking, you'll want to monitor your thoughts for their quality, discarding any ideas that are negative or not in your best interest. Remember to let go of any doubts or fears about your capability to succeed. You'll need to train yourself to discourage thoughts of worry, undue criticism, or bias.

MAJOR CAREER MASTER CONCEPTS

The following six concepts will help you improve your mindset, no matter what career season you happen to be experiencing.

MASTER CONCEPT ONE: THE CAREER MASTER

In you resides all the potential you need to succeed in your career. By recognizing that you have what it takes to achieve your career dreams, you become the career master—in charge of your own employment destiny. You'll gain insights to solve complex career challenges, make good employment decisions, and take appropriate steps toward job change. Your inner wisdom will assist you in your search for career fulfillment in addition to using the time-honored tools of an updated résumé, effective interviewing methods, and career exploration techniques to cover all the bases in the employment game.

The career master concept is a unique way of thinking that can help you reach job fulfillment. All you need to do is to tap into your own self-awareness, practice career master thinking, and take the appropriate action steps toward achievement. Now here are some of the ways that you can increase your self-awareness, and, in so doing, get the career master in you to come alive.

HEART'S WISDOM. By listening to the wisdom of your heart, often called *intuition*, you'll receive clear indications of the next action needed on your path to success. For your heart's wisdom to be most effective, you must learn to recognize the importance of the messages inherent in your own strong feelings or hunches.

INNER CONTEMPLATION. Spending time in quiet meditation can help you stay in touch with your inner wisdom on a regular basis. Your inner guide has access to knowledge unavailable to your conscious mind, and the primary way you can receive that knowledge is by practicing daily inner contemplation. The first inner contemplation for you to try is introduced in Master Concept Six.

MASTER CONCEPT TWO: YOUR SIGNPOSTS TO SUCCESS

Know that you have never made a career mistake in your life. No matter what your employment past has been like up until now, you will have gained valuable knowledge from your experience—even if it's the knowledge of what you won't do in the future or warning signs that you will look out for!

Chastising yourself for past actions wastes a lot of mental energy. Why spend time worrying about a career challenge or decision you made last week, last year, or twenty years ago? By the same token, projecting too far ahead into the future without taking care of today can be counterproductive. Your mental focus should remain in the present moment, even as you make plans for your future.

One very good reason to stay focused on the now is to take advantage of the many signs and opportunities that are presented to you. For example, an overheard conversation about a job opening might lead you to a new career, or you might meet someone on the spur of the moment who may end up to be your next client, or you may read in a newspaper about an organization that you might investigate further only to discover your ideal position within it. If you are not acutely aware of what's going on around you right now, both in your career and in a job search, you could miss the cue you've been waiting for.

Master Concept Three: Loosen Your Grip on Success

Loosening your grip on success is one of the most important things you can do as you proceed along your career path. When you focus so intently on the future, you're ignoring the work you're doing at the moment. Thus, your work will suffer and your future goals will be self-sabotaged. By detaching from an expectation of career achievement, you can adjust smoothly and quickly to job changes, no matter how fast they come at you. When you can lose a job and know that something better is coming around the corner, you've got the basic idea of how to loosen your grip on success.

Debra spent years with a single-minded focus on attaining success in the music industry. In that very competitive business, she found that she wasn't making the headway she desired after chasing her dream for more than a decade. Eventually she decided to switch gears. Her current career as a dental assistant, although not glamorous, suits her much better. Debra continues to enjoy her music as a hobby.

The Spring person, for example, needs to be flexible as new opportunities either pan out or lead to some other career path entirely. A high level of enthusiasm combined with a loosened grip on success will serve the Spring individual well through abrupt career changes. Your profession will go through cycles, and forcing a career to fit at a time when it isn't meant to be is like Cinderella's stepsister trying to squeeze her large foot into that dainty slipper. It just won't happen.

It May Be the Perfect Time to Move On. How do you know when it's time to redirect your career goals? At what point do you decide to move on to Plan B? It's important to realize that there may be a reason why circumstances don't go your way, no matter how hard you've been trying.

If you're a Spring person, you're putting a lot of energy into making things happen in your chosen field. Maybe you're toiling away with little to show for it, and the door to your desired opportunity doesn't seem to want to open right now. This may mean that another career move may be more beneficial for you at present.

Janet, a young woman fresh out of high school, had always wanted to be an actress. In the Spring of her career, she began following her dream by attending acting classes and volunteering for charity stage events. In a matter of months, Janet progressed to roles in community theater plays. Five years later, she was performing at the same local venues with no apparent way to go further in her acting career.

Because pursuing her acting career had hit a dead end, Janet decided to change directions. She went to college to get her teaching certificate. Far from feeling sad about this major career change, Janet knew that she could continue her acting as a sideline for now. By entering the teaching profession, Janet found a new way to use her skills in service to others.

Sometimes it's tough to know when it's the right time to cut your losses and move on to a new endeavor. Your feelings will offer helpful clues. Feeling down or frustrated can be a warning sign that action is needed. Some choose to disregard their hunches or deep-seated feelings and in so doing miss important opportunities. When you're alert to your own inner wisdom, you realize that feelings of dissatisfaction indicate that something is wrong and that it may be time to change jobs or careers—or take steps to improve your current situation.

Fear can keep you from making appropriate and necessary career transitions. Many Autumn people are afraid of change, but the act of maintaining the status quo just because it's easier has a way of keeping life on the stale side. What's the worst thing that could happen if you took the bull by the horns and went for your career dream? Consider a job move carefully, and plan wisely, but don't overlook the wisdom of your own heart. It may be telling you to go for it!

Financial challenges can arise when you're on the wrong employment track as well. Having the right job enables your energy to flow in a more positive fashion, resulting in vigor and enthusiasm for your work. Loving what you do promotes excellence in job performance, thus helping to attract financial gains, and your work life doesn't have to be one of simply tolerating a job for a steady paycheck. So if you are on a roller-coaster ride with your money and you are experiencing job dissatisfaction, note that there may be a connection and consider transitioning to an employment path with fewer struggles and more satisfaction.

MASTER CONCEPT FOUR: THE SOUL WEB

The Soul Web is the hypothetical invisible net that unites you with the other individuals in your private and professional circles. You are linked to others through social interactions, shared interests, and occupational pursuits. Your own personal network of acquaintances, friends, and relatives becomes a means of drawing even more people, things, and circumstances into your life. Your circle of contacts increases with every effort you make to expand your career—and the personal and professional relationships, or Soul Web, you develop are the primary avenues by which you will make career success happen.

You already know that networking is an effective method to create new business and to make important career contacts. Think of the Soul Web as an ever-expanding set of connections that allows you to build new career opportunities beyond your own local network.

Because your own network is a microcosm of the larger global network, the actions you take toward others are extremely significant. According to social psychologist Stanley Milgram's theory of six degrees of separation, where a chain of as few as six people could connect us to anyone else in the world, you are closer than you may think in having an effect on the world in general. That's why it can be crucial to practice the Golden Rule ("Treat others as you would wish to be treated") in your career dealings—your compassion, kindness, and generosity can have far-reaching consequences, indeed.

The Soul Web, as it relates to your career aspirations, could be represented as shown in Figure 1.

The Soul Web links you to other individuals in the world. On every step of your career journey the Soul Web, via your own personal and work connections, brings you feedback.

Feedback from the Soul Web, which can be extremely varied, will determine your next course of action. For instance, there may

✿ FIGURE 1 THE SOUL WEB

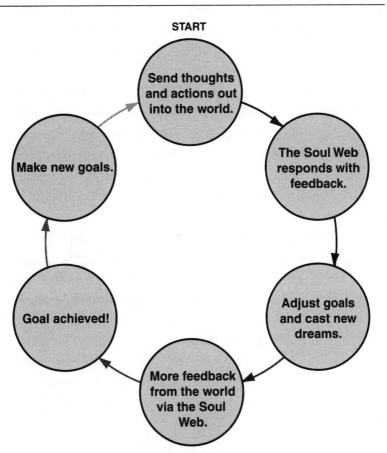

be a position you really want and your résumé is in the company's hands. When they call you to set up an interview, that is feedback from the Soul Web—you've reached the first of a series of steps to attain that job. If you don't get the position, that is further feedback that perhaps you should reexamine your résumé, experience, interviewing techniques, or the kinds of jobs you're applying for.

By paying attention to how the world reacts to you, you'll gain insight into how to make necessary changes in the way you operate in your work environment—and you'll be ready to take new action steps accordingly.

MASTER CONCEPT FIVE: LET GO OF YOUR EGO

The ego has an important role in your life. It helps you to maintain a sense of separateness from others. Taken to an extreme, however, a person's ego can manifest feelings of superiority, coldness, and selfishness.

An out-of-control ego is not a pretty sight. Symptoms of an ego needing adjustment are rudeness, road rage, impatience, bossiness, aggression, and overspending. A Hollywood star demanding a dressing room filled with chocolate-covered berries, champagne, a thousand silk purple pillows, and two Shetland ponies is an extreme example of an excessive ego; however, average folks in typical jobs may also exhibit overblown egos.

You Summer people in particular may need to tone down your ego, especially as you experience higher and higher degrees of success. To rise to the top of any profession is a significant and commendable accomplishment. The wise Summer person uses a leadership position as part of an overall path of service, instead of giving in to the ego's steady pleas for more of everything.

There is a practical reason to keep your ego under strict management. It is next to impossible to sustain happiness when your ego rules the roost. As long as the ego has its way, you will seek the next pleasure, and the next after that, to obtain a shallow version of contentment. True happiness rests in inner peace and fulfillment, based on a quiet serenity gained through self-knowledge and experience. Taming your ego is the best thing you could ever do for career and personal growth.

This next quiz will help you to determine the status of your ego. You'll want to discover if your ego is dominant or tamed in your own life. By finding out which way the ego wind blows, you'll be able to make the needed adjustments.

HOW'S MY EGO?

Take this quiz to see how your ego measures up. Put a check mark on the appropriate line.

	That's Me	Not Me
1. I find myself envying other people's looks.	_____	_____
2. I often snap at other people.	_____	_____
3. It's a dog-eat-dog world, and the most aggressive dog gets the bone!	_____	_____
4. I've had my share of speeding tickets.	_____	_____
5. I enjoy winning and get upset when I lose.	_____	_____
6. I need people to give me compliments.	_____	_____
7. Most people I meet aren't as talented as I am.	_____	_____
8. My friends are important people— or they aren't my friends.	_____	_____

	That's Me	Not Me
9. I rarely hold the door open for someone behind me.	_____	_____
10. Most rules don't apply to me.	_____	_____

ANSWER KEY

Score 1 point for every "That's Me."

If you scored between 0 and 2 points, congratulations! You have a healthy ego.

If you scored between 3 and 6 points—ego alert! See the "Ego Control Guidelines" in this chapter to head off potential problems.

If you scored between 7 and 10 points, run, don't walk, to the "Ego Control Guidelines" to tame your runaway ego.

EGO CONTROL GUIDELINES. Now that you've taken the quiz, you have a good idea of where you stand. If your score indicates that you need to practice keeping your ego in check, study the following guidelines. Make sure you follow through by practicing the recommendations on a regular basis. Having an out-of-control ego will not add to your career fulfillment and likely will create obstacles to your success. By taking steps to tame your ego, you'll be doing yourself a big favor in terms of your eventual professional achievement.

- *For general ego control:* Practice the inner contemplation series in this book.

- *If you tend to gossip or to criticize:* Catch critical thoughts when they occur and modify them.

- *If you have problems with road rage or aggressive behavior:* Use the inner contemplation techniques. Concentrate on your sense of connectedness to others (Soul Web).

- *If you see yourself as better than others:* Remember that everyone has special talents. Study the Soul Web concept.

- *If you are rude to strangers, friends, and family:* Try to monitor and modify your thoughts to prompt more positive behavior. Rudeness stems from a lack of connection with others.

- *If you need compliments and attention to feel good about yourself:* Write down a list of positive statements about yourself and reflect on them. How you feel about yourself shouldn't be based on the opinions of others.

- *If you crave more and more material goods, such as cars, money, clothes:* Realize that you already have abundance—without all the goodies. Examine why you believe you need a profusion of material objects to be happy. Feelings of abundance exist on the inside, not in exterior trappings.

MASTER CONCEPT SIX: PRACTICE INNER CONTEMPLATION

Setting aside time for inner contemplation is one of the most valuable steps you can take to develop your career master thinking skills. By spending quiet moments alone in your home or in nature, you set the stage for self-discovery and provide yourself with the time to make a thorough and valuable assessment of your career goals. This will lead to insights on the next steps you need to take to achieve these goals. It may be easy to say that you don't have enough hours in the day to devote to meditation. In reality, inner contemplation takes about twenty minutes a day and will result in an easier flow in all your personal and career situations.

The following is the first of many inner contemplation exercises in this book for you to use to gain more insight about your career path.

Inner Contemplation: The Career Master

Get seated comfortably, and take a few slow breaths to relax. Observe your thoughts as they go through your mind, and just let them continue to flow without judgment. After a few minutes of quiet observation, focus your mind on a vision of yourself as the career master—confident, competent, and in full command of your career path. See yourself working productively in your dream career. Notice your feelings as you perform a job you love. Imagine how you might reach your dream career. Relax and let the answer come to you in its own way. Don't be concerned if you don't receive any great revelations. Sitting quietly in meditation is still a great way to relieve stress.

Your Career Master Thinking Plan

Now that you've been introduced to the career master concepts, it's time to make your own career master thinking plan. Taking the time to plot your course will give you a helpful reference that you can use each day, as you work toward fulfilling your authentic career path. Think about the career master concepts found throughout this chapter and how they relate to you and the season of your career. Make a list of the specific steps you can take to enhance your career master thinking skills, identify and reach goals, and maintain a positive attitude and ego.

3

THE MIRROR ON YOUR CAREER

The one whose judgment counts most in your life is the one
staring back in the glass.

—Unknown

WHAT SKILLS DO YOU bring to a job? What do you enjoy doing? If you could have any career in the world, what would it be? What traits or abilities could you improve? Self-awareness is the key to selecting a career goal—you have to know what makes you tick before you can be sure which job will be right for you. If you want a career that brings you joy, excitement, and satisfaction in life, you will want to do some serious inner searching for answers to the above questions.

WHO ARE YOU, ANYWAY?

Take a group of ten people who know you, and what will you find? Everyone will have something different to say about you, depending on how well they know you, and their various perceptions, biases, and memories. Though they may not tell you directly how they feel about you, their actions will reflect their beliefs. One acquaintance may think you are boisterous and aggressive, while a friend may believe you are outgoing and straightforward. Will the real "you" please stand up?

Most of our lives (unless we are fortunate enough to learn some basic truths), we drift along, swayed by the opinions of others. To define ourselves, we use the feedback we receive from family, friends, and strangers. In addition, we tend to judge ourselves by what we see in movies, magazines, and television. In fact, much of our sense of identity seems to be derived from outside sources.

Maybe you've had a family member say that the career you really wanted was something that you couldn't achieve based on what they thought about you and your talents. Without a strong sense of self-awareness and a thorough understanding of what makes you tick as an individual, you could find yourself floundering in a sea of other people's opinions. Taking other people's beliefs about you to heart can keep you from following your own best career path.

THE HOUSE OF MIRRORS

Imagine yourself in a house of mirrors, a place where you can change your shape at will. All you've got is you and hunks of metal, reflective glass, and your imagination; you can observe yourself transformed into many different shapes and sizes. In one mirror, you look as thin as a pencil, while in another, you appear about one foot tall and five feet wide. What you see depends on the mirror and on how you position yourself. Each mirror tells a different story about you, but no one mirror can capture your true essence.

Your career path can be compared to a house of mirrors—complete with confusing turns, bizarre reflections, and unique distortions. It may be difficult to figure out which reflection represents your genuine path, as you try out various jobs to find the one with the perfect fit. One career after another may seem as if it doesn't quite suit you, much as the pencil-thin vision of you in the mirror doesn't match your internal picture of yourself.

Although your path through the career seasons may not be as confusing as a trip through a house of mirrors, there is a similarity between the two. In both cases, you'll need to know the "real" you—your skills, talents, and interests—to make any progress. Knowing who you are will help you choose and sustain a rewarding career, in addition to helping you achieve personal satisfaction in all other facets of your life. Because you will never see yourself in any mirror the way others see you, your task is to know yourself so well that no reflection will fool you into believing you're something you're not.

HOLDING UP THE MIRROR

To get a clear reflection of where you stand at the present time let's now hold up a mirror on your career. Look deeply into the glass, and see what it reveals. By shining a mirror on your career path thus far, you'll be able to see the road ahead more easily.

THE MIRROR ON YOUR CAREER WORKSHEET

Get a sheet of paper and answer these questions as honestly as you can. If you currently are not working, answer as it pertains to your last job.

1. Who propelled you toward (or what circumstances brought you to) your current (or last) job or career?

2. At first, did this career seem a good choice? Explain.

√3. If you are still in this career, what has kept you there? What refuels your decision to return day after day?

√4. What steps can you take now to effect change if you want a new job or career?

√5. Do you intend to remain in your present job?

6. What, if anything, is the one thing that dampens your enthusiasm for your job? Do you see a way to rekindle that enthusiasm?

√7. If you could decide all over again, would this be your career choice? Explain.

√8. If you could leave your present job today, with no strings attached and regardless of compensation, what would you choose to do?

9. Do you think your personal history limits your choices and career mobility? If so, how?

By completing the worksheet, you've taken the first step toward increased self-awareness. Introspection is the primary way you will find out how far you've come in your working life; it can also tell you where you're headed. Are you in a job that reflects the authentic you?

If you have not been working in a field that suits your image in the career mirror, it's time to figure out why it isn't so. With your worksheet in hand, take a look at your responses to questions 3, 4, 5, and 8. If you answered truthfully, your replies will be illuminating. Now that you know what motivates you to stay in your present work, is it enough to keep you there? What's stopping you from taking the steps you must take in order to find career fulfillment?

REFLECTIONS THROUGHOUT THE SEASONS

While in the Spring career season, you'll need to be clear about what you want in a career, what you have to offer, and how you will set and achieve your goals. Take in the landscape, survey all the possibilities for growth, and identify the specific steps you need to take as well as a time frame for reaching your goals.

You, Summer friend, are far down the road of success and have tried and mastered most aspects of your job. Your reflection in the glass may very well be one of self-satisfaction. However, if ego has gained the upper hand, your image may be exaggerated and larger than life. Be sure to keep your pride in check as you continue to succeed.

The uneventful figure in the mirror is the Autumn traveler. Unless and until something sets off your motivation for career renewal, you will continue to remain comfortable in a job that offers little challenge or new opportunity. When you find yourself in a job that you've long ago outgrown, and when you desire challenge over comfort, it may be time to consider taking action to reinvigorate your career.

The one common thread Winter individuals have is the need for self-awareness at this time of perhaps profound change. No matter what your situation, as a Winter person you now have the opportunity to plan for a period of major renewal. Changes may be coming so fast in your career and personal life that your reflection in the mirror captures only uncertainty. Now is the time to become clear about what you want and how to begin to accomplish it.

INNER CONTEMPLATION: SHINING A MIRROR ON YOUR CAREER

The goal of this exercise is to put your current career in perspective to identify specific moments of satisfaction and dissatisfaction. Relax in a comfortable chair, and focus the mirror in your mind on the events that occurred at work this past week. (If you are not employed right now, think back to your last job.) Think about the times you felt glad to be at work. What were you doing when you felt joyful? Were you interacting with coworkers, or were you in the middle of a challenging project? Think about those moments when you felt job satisfaction.

Now consider those times at work last week when you were not as pleased with your job. What was going on during your moments of dissatisfaction? Were you bored with having no new assignments to do? Or were you rushed because your job was so busy? Reflect on the reason for your frustration at work.

Can you spot a pattern in the episodes you've examined? In your mind's mirror reflection, you might have been able to discover what you like best about your work—and what you could do without on the job. With that information, you could take steps to prevent future annoying situations, and strive to increase the satisfying ones. Should you discuss with your supervisor constructive ways to eliminate these annoying situations or is it time to look for a new job altogether?

YOUR DEFINITION OF SUCCESS

The way you define success is critical to your happiness in any career endeavor. The word *success* may mean something different to you than it does to your neighbor. Whether you desire recognition for your talents, a large salary, personal satisfaction, or the simple pleasure of serving others, your own version of success will be the only one worth seeking.

Earning a large paycheck won't fit your definition of success if money doesn't matter that much to you. By the same token, seeing your name in lights could be the only true marker of career success you've ever considered. Your definition of what success means to you will be a paramount factor in identifying what steps to take to achieve it.

If you land in work that does not fulfill your own success definition, you may end up in an Autumn or Winter season, without a rewarding profession. By taking the time to find out what success means to you, you'll be able to match your success needs with a job that provides them. As part of your self-awareness plan, spend a few moments on this next quiz to find out the meaning of success in your life.

SUCCESS MEANS TO ME . . .

To find out your definition of success, answer each of the following questions by writing either T (True) or F (False) on the blank line.

1. Success means personal satisfaction on the job, regardless of material gain. _____

2. I'm a success if I rise to the top of my profession. _____

3. Having a happy personal life is all the success I need. _____

4. Career success is measured by the size of my paycheck. _____

5. If I'm recognized as a good person and a competent, caring worker, I'm satisfied. _____

6. My income plays only a minor role in my overall happiness. _____

7. Helping others reach their personal goals and potential brings me a great feeling of success. _____

8. To me, having the car I've always dreamed of is the signpost of success. _____

9. Success is having a happy marriage and caring relationships. _____

10. My faith in a higher power is more important than any monetary success I might enjoy. _____

11. As long as I make the effort, I am successful, even though I might not achieve my goal. _____

12. It's important for me to live in a spacious house with lots of amenities. _____

13. I'm not a success until I've reached a certain level of fame. _____

14. You should only get married to someone who has the same or greater financial assets than you do. _____

15. I'm not getting rich from my job, but I do this work for the enjoyment of it. _____

16. I'm usually recognized for my talents and achievements on the job. _____

17. I need a career that affords me enough free time to pursue my hobbies and interests. _____

18. I haven't achieved enough in my career to make me happy. _____

19. I need enough money to buy the luxury items that I deserve. _____

20. Advancing my career in the fastest way possible is my main objective. _____

21. I would be devastated if I didn't ever reach my career goals. _____

Your Success Factor Key

Add up your totals for your true and false answers, and read the key to determine what success means to you.

Question	True	False	Points
1.	1 point	3 points	_____
2.	3 points	1 point	_____
3.	1 point	3 points	_____
4.	3 points	1 point	_____
5.	1 point	3 points	_____
6.	1 point	3 points	_____
7.	1 point	2 points	_____
8.	3 points	1 point	_____
9.	1 point	2 points	_____
10.	1 point	3 points	_____
11.	1 point	3 points	_____
12.	3 points	1 point	_____
13.	3 points	1 point	_____
14.	3 points	1 point	_____
15.	1 point	3 points	_____
16.	3 points	2 points	_____
17.	1 point	2 points	_____
18.	3 points	1 point	_____
19.	3 points	1 point	_____
20.	3 points	1 point	_____
21.	3 points	1 point	_____

GRAND TOTAL: _____

ANSWER KEY

If you scored between 21 and 33 points, personal satisfaction is your definition of success.

If you scored between 34 and 46, you have a balance between your need for personal satisfaction and your desire for fame and fortune.

If you scored 47 or more points, your need to achieve wealth and status overrides every other factor.

Now you should be clear on the success factors that drive you. Knowing your achievement requirements can be a valuable first step in actually satisfying those needs. Are you currently in a work situation that matches your success profile?

SUCCESS THROUGHOUT THE SEASONS

Earmarks of success for you as a Spring individual could include attaining the position you sought in a new career field, learning the ropes of your job, or picking up additional skills that could bring career advancement later on. Because you are focused in a season that corresponds with new growth and expanding opportunity, reaching the top of your profession at this point may be a little premature. You would do well to gain experience and take note of how well you fit in with your work surroundings at this juncture, rather than holding any expectation of grand financial reward or rapid advancement. Patience is the key here, as you lay the groundwork for a career peak to come in the Summer season.

If you're a Summer individual, you might be on your way up the corporate ladder or already at the top. Your signs of success may consist of material assets and the prestige of an important job title, or they could include the personal satisfaction of high accomplishment. No matter what your career field, if you have reached the point where you feel successful, you are in Summer.

As a Summer person, you're in the season of a potential runaway ego that can drive you further and further into a materialistic lifestyle—and out of touch with your career master. Keep in mind that career success does not guarantee personal happiness. Take the appropriate steps to balance your life in and out of the office.

A sign of accomplishment for you as an Autumn person can be successfully sorting out where you wish to go from here. You can win in Autumn by deeply scrutinizing your career wants and needs, evaluating the skills and strengths you have at your disposal, and clarifying your professional goals and what it would take to achieve them.

Perhaps after careful consideration you'll find that you're happiest just staying in your current position, for reasons of financial security and not wanting to stray from your comfort zone. So be it—and your definition of success will make clear that you've done what was best for you all along.

Your success during the Winter season could be based on a number of factors, not the least of which is a steadfast resolve to make a new start. You'll be a winner in Winter if you are able to maintain a positive attitude; keeping a bright spirit will charge your mental batteries while you're going through times of great transition. In addition, succeeding in Winter depends on careful preparation for your next career chapter or, if you have no intention of beginning a new career at this point in your life, a successful Winter season means personal fulfillment and the knowledge that you've made the right choice at this period in your life.

IT'S ALL ABOUT YOU

You were born with a unique set of abilities, and through the years you've honed your talents and acquired new ones. In addition, there are certain jobs you would do for free because they interest you so much, while you would avoid other positions no matter what they pay, because they don't appeal to you. There is a career that suits you to a tee, and you'll find it if you truly seek it.

Let's take a look at your abilities and job interests now. Think carefully about your answers on the next worksheet—the more accurate they are, the more insight you'll gain into the most fascinating person of all: you.

IT'S ALL ABOUT ME

Answer the following questions as honestly as you can.

1. In my opinion, my best skill of all is

   _____.

2. To work in my chosen field, a skill I may need to improve is

   _____.

3. Some abilities I've acquired in other jobs are

   _____

   _____.

4. Other people tell me I'm good at these skills:

   _____

   _____.

5. If someone were to hand me my dream career today, it would be

   _____.

6. One job I really enjoyed was

   _____

   because

   _____.

7. You couldn't pay me enough to work at

   _____

   because

   _____.

8. My ideal job contains these characteristics:

   _____ .

9. The one thing I *must* have in a job is

   _____ .

10. When I see these warning signs, I know I need to move on to a new job:

    _____ .

Now that you've put your skills and career interests down on paper, you can begin to obtain an authentic image in your career mirror by reviewing your responses. No one else can identify what will satisfy your career fulfillment needs better than *you* can. By doing some intensive self-reflection, you'll surely see a true likeness looking back at you from the glass. If you assessed your abilities and interests accurately, you're ready to blend them into a career that you'll love.

WHAT'S YOUR NET WORTH?

Your true net worth has very little to do with your financial holdings. Instead, your intrinsic worth is all about the inner qualities and philosophy of life that you carry around with you each day—the fundamental character traits that brand you for what you really are. In your mirror reflection, what do you see? Do you gaze into the eyes of someone you can respect, or does your likeness produce feelings of dislike, shame, or regret?

It's important to point out that your net worth is continually in the process of changing as you grow as a person throughout your lifetime. With increased years and/or spiritual growth may come advanced wisdom, with corresponding attention to values that are independent of material gain. This higher level of inner wisdom will sustain you when your ship comes in, and when it goes out to sea again.

Take this quiz for insight into an aspect of grave importance—your own inner worth. You'll discover your level of inner wisdom and values, which are priceless aspects in developing your career path of service.

WHAT'S YOUR NET WORTH?

For each of the following statements, write T (True) or F (False) on the blank line.

1. I use my skills in positive service to others. _____

2. I make a point to give my best in any relationship. _____

3. Occasionally I try to get people to do things my way because my way is best. _____

4. I'm generous with my time and money. _____

5. I usually get irritated if I don't get what I want. _____

6. I don't have a lot of time to help people with their personal crises. _____

7. My positive attitude keeps me afloat in tough situations. _____

8. People tell me that I brighten their days. _____

9. While I'm not a deceptive person, sometimes I have to tell a white lie to advance my career. _____

10. I believe that things happen for a reason. _____

11. If I have problems with people on the job, it's rarely my fault. _____

12. Honesty is my best policy when I do business. _____

13. I tend to get frustrated if I have to wait in line for anything. _____

14. When it comes to achieving career success, I want to advance quickly up the ladder. _____

15. People like to come to me for advice. _____

16. I accept people just the way they are—I don't believe in judging them. _____

17. Some individuals can't be forgiven for what they've done. _____

18. I really feel for people who are suffering. _____

19. Getting ahead in my career is the most important thing. _____

20. Sometimes I can annoy people by my actions at work. _____

21. My family comes first and my career second. _____

22. I always choose to believe the best about people. _____

23. Once in a while, my temper gets me in trouble. _____

24. Often, I feel hassled by people. _____

25. If a friend has a problem, I offer my assistance without hesitation. _____

26. On the whole, life just hasn't been fair to me. _____

Your Net Worth

Add your total points to find out your net worth.

Question	True	False	Points
1.	1 point	2 points	_____
2.	1 point	2 points	_____

Question	True	False	Points
3.	2 points	1 point	_____
4.	1 point	2 points	_____
5.	2 points	1 point	_____
6.	2 points	1 point	_____
7.	1 point	2 points	_____
8.	1 point	2 points	_____
9.	2 points	1 point	_____
10.	1 point	2 points	_____
11.	2 points	1 point	_____
12.	1 point	2 points	_____
13.	2 points	1 point	_____
14.	2 points	1 point	_____
15.	1 point	2 points	_____
16.	1 point	2 points	_____
17.	2 points	1 point	_____
18.	1 point	2 points	_____
19.	2 points	1 point	_____
20.	2 points	1 point	_____
21.	1 point	2 points	_____
22.	1 point	2 points	_____
23.	2 points	1 point	_____
24.	2 points	1 point	_____

Question	True	False	Points
25.	1 point	2 points	_____
26.	2 points	1 point	_____
		GRAND TOTAL:	_____

If you scored 30 or below, you have a lot to offer others through your career of service. Your philosophy of life is positive and embraces compassion for people, honesty in your dealings, and patience in achieving your career goals. Your high net worth will hold you in good stead all along your employment path. Congratulations on reaching a level that takes some people their whole lives to achieve.

If your score is between 31 and 35, you are on the right track to combining your own goals with a career of service to others. Your image in the mirror might show a person who is balanced and frequently moving forward in the area of self-improvement.

If your score is 36 and above, you might want to take a look at your philosophy of life and the way in which you live it. Although perhaps you have the best of intentions, you may be taking some unhelpful shortcuts along your career path. If you are of service to others while seeking to fulfill your own employment dreams, you will be rewarded many times over as you progress through your career. Change may be necessary at this point so that you can become the person you want to be when you look into your career mirror.

WHAT DO YOU SEE IN THE MIRROR?

By now you've gone through the Mirror on Your Career worksheets and quizzes, and you've gained a new understanding of where you are in your career cycle—and where you are headed. You've examined the steps you took to get to your current career, and reviewed your job choices. You've looked at your definition of success, your skills and interests, and your intrinsic net worth.

You've gone through the process of putting your career experiences through a comprehensive scrutiny to see an authentic reflection in the glass. Take a look right now into a mirror. Are you seeing the real you, with all of your many facets, talents, and positive qualities?

Now let's find out how to make your job goals come to life. You can achieve your professional objectives by using a little goal magic. In the next chapter, you'll learn how to get your career dreams moving forward.

4

GOALS FOR ALL SEASONS

*Even if you're on the right track, you'll get run over if you
just sit there.*

——WILL ROGERS

DOES THIS SOUND FAMILIAR? "I'll take any job that's offered to
me—I want a change!" Without a specific and realistic goal in
mind, it will be a lot more difficult to bring yourself just the right
job opportunity. When you pinpoint a goal, your mind focuses on
your objective—your brain becomes increasingly aware of what it
takes to achieve the goal—so you are able to take appropriate
action to reach it in the swiftest possible manner.

If you haven't thought carefully enough about your career goals,
you may find yourself at a loss for words when you're asked what
kind of job you're looking for. By not targeting a specific career, you

run the risk of remaining at the status quo—and not working in your dream job. That said, it is not an easy task to identify the career in which you will both excel and find personal fulfillment. Never fear, no matter which career season you're currently going through, the exercises in this chapter will help you zero in on the career of your dreams.

YOUTHFUL DREAMS

No matter how much you love your job, you probably have some days during which you find yourself wondering what it would be like to do something entirely different for a living. These imaginings may stem from the interests and ambitions you had when you were young. Some of us took our early dreams to heart and realized them, while others chose more practical and stable career paths.

Close your eyes and take yourself back in time to when you were five or six years old. Remember your childhood ambitions, and what you wanted to be when you grew up. Did you want to be an astronaut, doctor, or police officer? Let those early memories flood back into the present time, until you recollect the career goal or goals you had as a youngster.

In retrospect, did you grow up to do the work of your youthful dreams? If not, what prompted you to shift job gears? Is your current occupation related in some unique way to what you said you wanted to be when you grew up? Take a few minutes now to write down your first career ambitions and the results of those dreams.

After examining your childhood career dreams, you should have some clarification as to why your career path went the way it did. If you are dissatisfied in your present position, you may want to think about how valid your childhood dreams are to you today. Is a career change appropriate? Are there ways in which you can incorporate your current experience with your true interest?

SET A GOAL, GET A GOAL!

If you're like most people you've been told all your life to set goals. Well-meaning relatives and teachers may have attempted to guide you by emphasizing the importance of choosing and achieving the right goals. They knew that, with no career ambition, you were likely to coast along in life taking the path of least resistance. While going with the flow is perfectly fine, the practice of setting goals can keep you moving to fulfill your highest potential. Be a goal-getter!

WHAT IS A GOAL?

A goal is a desire that you pursue and something you must take action to realize. Your goal must be specific, realistic, and measurable. But most of all, your career objective must be something that you are willing to expend major amounts of time and energy on. So be sure you really want what you think you want.

A goal has definite steps. If you have an extremely ambitious aim, you'll want to break down your target into smaller chunks to make it doable. In addition, it's important to give yourself a sense of accomplishment by keeping track of each step's success. Your motivation stays high when you can see the positive results of your efforts.

The bottom line for any goal may be: how much do you want it? The truth is that you can achieve your target if you have the skills, desire, and dedication to do so. That is not to say that you will accomplish your aim overnight—it could take a period of years to make it in your field, depending on the various factors involved. Will your goal still hold its appeal if you don't achieve it within a short time?

THE ELUSIVE TARGET

Somewhere along the way, one of your goals may have slipped from your grasp. Maybe it was something you truly desired but weren't able to make happen at that point in your life. What made this target so elusive? Answer: you didn't focus on the goal and the specific steps you would need to take to achieve it. You either didn't want it badly enough, or you lacked the skills and knowledge to go the long haul, so you decided to do something else.

Brian thought his goal was to become a pharmacist. He had been intrigued with the idea of medicines and their effects since he was thirteen. Spurred on by his early success in science classes, Brian entered college with a pharmacy career uppermost in his mind.

At first, he tackled the requisite science courses with diligence, but as time went on, Brian managed to do everything but study. His grades fell, and his initial enthusiasm for a pharmacy career waned. Ultimately, as you might have guessed, Brian did not become a pharmacist.

What happened to Brian? Where did his dream go? Simply put, Brian did not stick with his early goal of a pharmacy career. Because the science coursework was more challenging than he would have liked, Brian lost interest in pharmacy altogether. He came to realize that he didn't have the passion it would take to become a pharmacist, so he moved on to another line of work that held more interest for him. Lucky for Brian, he had enough self-awareness to make a career change before getting entrenched in a profession that didn't suit him.

FALLING INTO THE BOTTOMLESS PIT

You may be in a career that you fell into for one or several reasons. Maybe the dream job that you were pursuing didn't appear—after giving up on your true ambition you may have grabbed the first opportunity for a paycheck. Or maybe you never had a serious career goal, and now you're paying the price by settling for a position far below your interests or capabilities.

It's perfectly OK to take a job that isn't your life's work. However, if you make a habit of staying too long in a place that really doesn't suit you, you do yourself no favors. There is no excuse to remain in a career that brings you few moments of joy. No amount of money, security, or prestige could ever make a job worthwhile if you're not happy in it.

The bottomless pit is that place where it seems like it's too late and too difficult to climb back out. Maybe when you first started in your present position, you thought that you'd spend only a couple of years, but those two years went by ages ago! Unless you make an effort to heave yourself over the top, you could remain trapped in a quagmire of missed opportunity and hopelessness. The bottomless pit isn't really bottomless after all—that's just an illusion. And because there *is* a way out of the pit, the solution lies within you to find it, by setting and following through on your goals.

THE TENDER TRAP

You might find yourself in a vocation that seems to offer you all the trappings of success you've ever wanted, with one limitation: it brings no career fulfillment. At first, you might have been entranced by the "bright lights, big city" nature of your work. The glamour of your job could have sidetracked you from taking your path of service. The money's right, the work's steady, and you're even good at what you do. So what if you don't love your job? The trap is sweet, isn't it? Or is it time to set a new career goal for yourself?

THE *TITANIC* EFFECT

Just like those travelers on the maiden voyage of the *Titanic*, full of excitement and a sense of history in the making, you may think that your career dreams are unsinkable. On the other hand, if you are pursuing a goal that does not match your skills, interests, and work preferences, you may end up sinking your career in the process.

In this case, your reflection in the career mirror might not be a genuine one at all. For example, let's say that you've been working in a company for several years, and some of your coworkers have been promoted—but not you. One reason for your lack of advancement might be that you don't fit well with that particular organization. In short, your goal of a promotion may never materialize—at least not in your present place of employment.

The best way of avoiding those employment icebergs is to check your career mirror regularly. What does your boss say about your job talents? Do your work evaluations correspond with what you think they should be? Without examining your mirror image, you could be fooling yourself into thinking that you've landed in the right position—when you might be better off in another career field altogether.

SETTING GOALS THROUGHOUT THE SEASONS

As a Spring career person, you are in the beginning stages of planning and growth. You have the opportunity to start fresh and to forge a solid foundation. The challenge, however, is that you will need to pay strict attention to your career choice. It's vital for you to keep frequent tabs on where you're going, and to monitor whether obtaining your goal is lighthearted or burdensome. A continual struggle is likely to mean that you are going against your own interests. If that's the case for you, you'll want to regroup, not continue to spit against the wind. Above all, maintain a positive outlook, even if things aren't going the way you had imagined, and keep your eyes open for the signposts that signal to you what your next step should be—whether that means taking on more responsibility in your current profession or moving on to gain experience with a different company.

You Summer people are used to a certain level of achievement. You may have reached a career pinnacle, or perhaps you're still climbing the ladder of job success—either way, you're a natural at following your ambitions.

Since you're already a master at setting goals within your career, this might be the time to look at aspects of your life outside of work. Have you maintained a good balance of activity in and out of the office? Are you content and satisfied with your personal life, as well as your professional one? If not, what steps can you take to achieve balance?

You, the individual traveling through the Autumn season, have an opportunity to transform your destiny for good by setting and achieving some fresh career goals. Once you decide to go down a new path, you should set goals that are clear, thoroughly considered, and reachable. By keeping your objectives fairly small and achievable, you'll gain the confidence you need to progress to new goals. Even though it may have been years since you've thought about setting goals for yourself, it's a skill that you can learn through practice and persistence.

As a Winter person, you are in a period of deep preparation for your next career phase. Now's the time to be practical and realistic in drafting fresh goals for yourself. Take a hard look at your work history, skills, and interests, and do some research on potential careers that grab your attention. You've reached an opportunity for growth even in the Winter of your career. The key is to realize that the Winter season is an important part of your positive transformation and career regeneration.

Regardless of your season, be sure the goal you set is the goal you really want. Often we pay lip service to other people's desires for us, when we have different ideas in mind altogether. You're the only one who knows which goals are most important to you, so choose them wisely. In addition, make sure you have thought out your career goal in detail, including how much time, money, and effort it would require for you to achieve it.

A LITTLE GOAL MAGIC

Already you've learned how to choose your thoughts wisely and to pick specific goals that suit your needs, talents, and career season. Once you've identified the job that you feel will be most fulfilling, you're ready to focus your attention on making it happen. Keep your goal in the forefront of your mind—think about your objective several times each day, and concentrate on the specific steps you need to take to achieve your goal.

According to Louis Pasteur, "Chance favors only the prepared mind." The more you learn about your ideal career through research and networking, the better chance you'll have of reaching your dream.

KEY ONE: BE CONSISTENT

The first key in accomplishing any career objective is to be consistent. It's all too common to start a new exercise program or other regimen with high hopes and promise, but after a few tries, let it slide into oblivion. The same is true for taking steps to land your next job or advance in your current position. The trick is to keep your momentum by continuing the goal achievement process every day. Remember, any positive habit requires extra concentration at first to get it established into your routine.

KEY TWO: CULTIVATE STAYING POWER

The real beauty of achieving goals is that the longer you persevere, the easier it gets. If you give up too soon you'll never know success—so why stop before you finish the race? Thomas Edison said, "Many of life's failures are people who did not realize how close they were to success when they gave up." Your patience in the hunt will be rewarded either by the accomplishment of your goal or the appearance of another road to travel—the only way to find out is to stay the course. Always remain positive and persistent in moving toward your goal.

KEY THREE: BEND IN THE WIND

If obstacles appear in your path, you should be flexible as to whether or not you want to continue pursuit of your particular objective. Just as a reed must bend in the wind or be broken, you'll want to monitor your progress and adjust your goals as you go along in your career.

KEY FOUR: ACCEPTING THE OUTCOME

Whether or not you attain your goal, you should accept the outcome. If you reach a high level of achievement, accept it as your well-deserved reward. If your goal does not reach fruition, understand that there's probably a good reason why you haven't accomplished your objective. As difficult as it may be to fall short of your dream, there's probably something better for you around the corner. The next goal you set should be to determine what that better dream is.

YOUR CAREER ACTION GUIDE

The world has two kinds of people—those who *do* and those who *watch*. If you're a watcher, you may learn a lot by watching the doers, but you won't get anywhere without taking action. Because every journey begins with a single step, even though your career path may be a long one, you should start now. Life is a process, not a destination—no matter in which season you find yourself, now is a good time to make your move.

To start the ball rolling on career growth and change, presuming that you have chosen a career target that fits your interests, skills, needs, and path of service, you're ready to make your dream a reality. There are many ways to go about plotting one's career course, and the following are just a few methods of career exploration that you could consider:

- Shadow someone on the job in your field of interest for a day.

- Conduct informational interviews to help you to decide on a specific field.

- Attend area job fairs.

- Use career centers in your city, including college and university centers, for testing and guidance.

- Network at your local unemployment agency's professionals club.

- Research possible careers at your local library and on the Internet.

- Use the *Occupational Outlook Handbook* (bls.gov/oco/) and the Occupational Information Network (onetcenter.org/).

- Practice your interviewing skills and research current trends on interviewing styles.

- Let friends, family, and acquaintances know you're looking for a new job.

- Read local business publications for news of your industry and review the new business listings.

- Consider your transferable skills as you plan for a future career.

- Be aware of the current trends in salary negotiation.

- Make sure your résumé is updated and free of typos.

Goal magic methods will help you find complete career fulfillment. As always, it's up to you to take the initiative and apply the techniques we share with you. We use these steps in our own practice every day, and they are very effective.

YOUR DREAM CAREER

On a separate sheet of paper, list your career goals by completing the following statements.

1. I am a successful _____ .
   (Fill in your desired job title.)

2. I plan to reach my career goal by _____ .
   (Fill in the desired date of achievement.)

3. I have several steps to take to reach my goal:
   My first action step: _____
   My second action step: _____
   My third action step: _____

4. My favorite affirmation or inspirational statement is

   _____ .

Review your goals daily to keep yourself focused and to refuel your motivation. Update this Dream Career Sheet frequently. After you accomplish your goal, write down a new career objective to take its place. The practice of setting new goals will ensure your continued growth in your career.

CAREER ACTION LOG

For best results, you should take at least two actions on your career goals per day, and record them on your Career Action Log. Keeping written track of the steps toward your career objectives can help you tremendously in planning follow-up actions. Another advantage to keeping a detailed log is that you won't have to remember when you took a step—it's all right there in front of you. Your Career Action Log should include these categories:

Date: _____

Action Taken: _____

Date to Follow-Up: _____

Follow-Up Action: _____

Your Dream Career Sheet and Career Action Log work in tandem to keep you on track and propel you forward to professional accomplishment. Use them every day for significant results.

ADJUST YOUR TARGET

Some targets are easier to accomplish than others. There may be times when little progress is evident—and other times when, by making thoughtful moves, you can achieve several goals very quickly. Whatever the case, be prepared to accept the flow of events on your journey to success.

When you get closer to your target, it might appear different than it did from a distance. You may want to modify or get rid of that particular goal if it no longer fits your idea of a fulfilling career.

Throughout the pursuit of your goal, if circumstances appear to be leading you to your target rather smoothly, you are very likely on the right track. Should you encounter situations of struggle or frustration, take some time to evaluate your career expedition and make any necessary adjustments to your plans. At a certain juncture, the cost of a goal (in terms of your energy, money, and time) may outweigh its potential benefit.

GOAL ACHIEVEMENT

Whether it takes you two months or twenty years to do it, and no matter how many times you have to adjust your target, eventually you reach a goal.

Perhaps your goal has been to return to college to finish your degree. After years of being out of school, you doubt that you'll be able to withstand the rigor of the academic scene once again. By breaking your larger goal into a series of smaller ones, you'll manage to obtain that diploma after all. Simply set your course and make adjustments as needed—it may take you longer to get your degree than you'd initially planned, but then again, great success does not always comply with your rigid schedule.

Your current goal may be to obtain a plum promotion. By plotting your action course and keeping a record of completed objectives, you'll be well on your way to advancement.

You cannot control all the elements involved in achieving a promotion, and there is no guarantee that your hard efforts will be rewarded in a step up the ladder—but the possibility of failure should never stop you from doing your best at all times.

5

THE FIFTEEN RULES FOR
STAYING POSITIVE

Very little is needed to make a happy life; it is all within yourself, in your way of thinking.
—Marcus Aurelius Antoninus

Now that you have the tools to create goal magic success, let's take a look at fifteen rules for staying positive, surefire ways to help keep you motivated and steady in your career climb. There is nothing more valuable than maintaining a positive outlook as you go through any career season.

How is it that some people can remain upbeat in the midst of personal and professional challenges? They probably have a strong faith in a purposeful universe and a solid understanding of how to control any negative thoughts that crop up.

Because the best-laid plans may not turn out exactly as you wish, it's important to remain flexible at every step of your career path. No direction you take is a mistake—it's all part of the learning process. Keep a positive attitude along the way, and make sure you follow these fifteen rules. Eventually your efforts will pay off.

1. IF IT DOESN'T SERVE YOU, DUMP IT!

The first rule of staying upbeat is crucial to your happiness in general. Although it may sound cold, you need to get rid of anything in your life that doesn't bring you happiness—including any relationships that bring on undue suffering. Whether it's a person, thing, or job that wears on your nerves, do yourself a favor—dump it!

Of course, blithely cutting and running from unwanted situations is not the answer. Before you make a major move, look closely at the circumstances that make you unhappy, and evaluate how you might alter them to feel more positive and fulfilled. When conditions get so challenging that you know it's time to take action, you should honor that feeling—and step away from the person, job, or situation.

You deserve to find a job that challenges and satisfies you. It is your right to be fulfilled in your career, but making that happen will take your own conviction that your perfect path of service is out there somewhere. If you believe that you merit only a boring, low-paying occupation, then that's what you'll get.

2. BE PATIENT—YOU'VE GOT THE REST OF YOUR LIFE

It may take you a lot longer than you wish to grab that brass ring. You can put out all the energy in the world to accomplish your career desires, but if your circumstances change and issues arise, you'll need nonattachment and patience to go with the flow of events.

Forcing circumstances to fit your preconceived notions will not bring you success any faster. In fact, desperately charging ahead when all signs indicate that you should wait will only serve to frustrate or discourage you. Your path to a summer in the sun may be winding instead of straight, long instead of short. After all, if you accomplished your dreams too easily, you wouldn't be nearly as pleased by the outcome, now would you?

In this age of not enough time and too much to do, patience is a lost art. Many individuals can barely tolerate waiting in lines, getting stuck on the road behind a slowpoke, or watching movies that have little action and a lot of leisurely dialogue. In the modern era, too much information coming at you too quickly is the norm. The accelerated pace of life has made us into people of limited attention span and minimal staying power.

You can develop more patience if you set your mind to it. By trimming your schedule down to the essentials, you'll have more time to relax, unwind, and put things in perspective. The result of taking time out can be a more long-term perspective on goal attainment.

Be careful that you don't make the mistake of confusing patience with ennui or fear of taking action—and don't use being patient as an excuse for not going forward with a necessary change.

3. KEEP THE RIGHT COMPANY

To stay positive, you should keep company only with those individuals who are positive, supportive, and enthusiastic. To associate with uplifting people will brighten your own spirit and encourage you to fulfill your career and personal goals.

An upbeat person will be quick to offer you a sincere "Good for you!" when informed of your accomplishments. A true friend will be eager to lend a hand or offer some genuine words of advice. You'll want to surround yourself with people of that exceptional variety—individuals with warm smiles and caring hearts.

You'll benefit from associating only with positive people—even if it means having very few close relationships. The number of friends that you have is not important—it's the quality of the relationships in your life that matters.

Conversely, if you surround yourself with egocentric, materialistic individuals with little concern for humanity, it's likely that your own growth could be stymied. By keeping the right company, your outlook has an excellent chance of remaining upbeat and optimistic.

4. BE ABUNDANT—IT'S NOT THE SIZE OF YOUR PAYCHECK THAT MATTERS

Abundance is your natural right, and with the proper mindset, it can always be yours. Worrying about where your next paycheck is coming from does you no good in keeping your mental attitude positive.

If you find yourself out of work in Winter, or with a small paycheck in the Spring of your career, it will take a leap of faith for you to see yourself as financially carefree. You may want to make some changes in your money situation by taking on a "survival" job outside your field to tide you over a short period in Winter. You could think about taking a second job or cutting back on your expenses as you maneuver through your Spring season.

Regardless of how you approach your money situation, abundance involves your spirit; it is *not* dependent upon what is in your wallet. Telling yourself that you always have what you need, if not always what you want, is a helpful affirmation to practice if you find yourself in a spot where the money is tighter than you'd like. By believing in your abundance before you see it materialize, you'll make it happen—that's both the paradox and the miracle.

5. BE AN ORIGINAL THINKER

Innovative creators are marked by a faith in their ability to come up with a new idea or product. The original thinker does not rely solely on the studies or opinions of others to make his own contribution.

Thinking for yourself is one of the most important aspects of living a life of happiness. Too often people take someone else's word instead of trusting their own judgment and feelings. One of the reasons you exist is to achieve your own ambitions, regardless of the goals a family member or friend may want you to pursue.

You can find just the right niche in a career field where you can really shine. To find that special place, trust your own dreams and guidance and move ahead down your career path on your own say-so, without becoming overly concerned about the wishes or opinions of others. The more you trust your own inner wisdom, the more you will be able to stay positive in a world that shows no sign of slowing down.

6. HANDLE THE STRESS OF CHANGE

To maintain a positive outlook on life, you'll need to control your reactions to stressful situations. It's crucial that you find methods to keep yourself calm and peaceful in the midst of changes and unexpected events.

All the career seasons have periods of potential stress. In Spring, when you are exploring uncharted career territory, you could be feeling more pressure to make a new job succeed. In Summer, you may experience increased tension due to all the hard work you're putting in to get ahead. Our Autumn friends might be under additional stress because of career indecision or feelings of being stuck. Winter folks have their own set of pressure-cooker events to manage, such as layoff, retirement, and other major life shifts.

For many people, change itself is stressful. But change is in our very nature. Career transitions are the norm of society, not the exception, and you can expect to change your work a number of times during your life. Because change will not be a stranger to you, handling its stress is crucial in maintaining a positive attitude.

If you're a person who procrastinates on work projects or school assignments until the last minute, you do yourself no favors. You may be adding unduly to your stress level by not taking care of your work when it needs to be done.

You can use a variety of methods for stress reduction, including taking time for yourself, sleeping and eating well, exercising, getting a regular massage, relaxing in nature, participating in recreational activities such as sports or yoga, and spending time with friends in uplifting conversation. All of these things can do wonders for your mood, and may open your eyes to other points of view you might not have considered.

7. RESOLVE CONFLICTS QUICKLY

Unresolved arguments or bad feelings can bring on stress and negativity that you don't need. Whether the difficulty begins with you or the other person, take early steps to eradicate an unpleasant situation. The result of your renewed peace of mind will be worth the effort you spend in smoothing over any relationship challenges.

Sometimes conflict can linger on for years, with neither side willing to give in, apologize, and move on. If this happens to you, the drain on your positive mental outlook may be very powerful.

The act of forgiving someone will help both parties involved by releasing the tension and beginning the healing process. Holding in your anger and behaving poorly toward another because you get a perverse pleasure out of seeing people suffer is not going to help you on your career path or in your personal life. If you are hanging on to a conflict from yesterday or the dimly remembered past, let it go, and your mental attitude will improve tremendously.

8. PUT YOURSELF FIRST

You're an exceptional individual. No one else can be exactly like you, with all of your unique qualities and attributes. And you have a career niche to fill, one that suits you to a tee.

Because you are so extraordinary, you'll want to treat yourself like the one-of-a-kind wonder you are. No more putting yourself last, no more sacrificing what you need for the wants of others. You come first. If you're not happy, those around you will be aware of it anyhow. An unfulfilled individual is not able to offer as much in a career or relationship as he or she might do otherwise. So take care of yourself—from pampering your body to buying yourself little gifts from time to time. You are worth it. Naturally, your attitude will be more upbeat as you treat yourself in the way you deserve— with respect and love.

9. WALK THE HIGH ROAD ON THE JOB

All too often when you turn on the evening news, you see evidence of people practicing the worst kinds of behavior at work. Stories about corporate fraud, executive dishonesty, and government scandals abound. Dishonesty may help a person achieve a dubious form of temporary fame, but it will not gain that person long-term satisfaction and happiness.

To keep a positive frame of mind, you'll want to be sure that you take the high road each day of your working life. There's nothing to be gained by stealing, lying, or gossiping in the workplace, and there may be everything to lose.

The higher path is to take responsibility for your words and deeds. Your mode of thinking crosses over into your conversation, thus you must take care with the language you use and the way you use it. Careless words can be damaging, both to your professional reputation and to your relationships with coworkers and other staff. Sending gossipy E-mails or spreading negative talk around the workplace can lead to a job environment that is uncomfortable and filled with tension.

By keeping to a higher path in your career, you'll establish a reputation for being an honest, responsible, and mature individual— one to be respected and admired. Having an excellent reputation can help you advance in your work because others perceive you as someone with integrity and strength of character.

10. MAKE TIME TO DO WHAT YOU REALLY WANT TO DO

You already know the keys to using your job time more effectively, from setting work priorities to listing tasks and appointments. But do you prioritize the other activities you do every day? Outside of work, do you find yourself obligated to attend too many events, meetings, and social functions? It may be time for a clean sweep of your calendar.

To find time to do what you really want to do, you need to do exactly that—spend your time in pursuits that bring you joy. Too often, our clients tell us that their lives are bogged down with activities that fill up their schedules, but offer little fulfillment. If you find yourself in that boat, then it's time to find a way out before you spring a leak.

For instance, instead of taking on all the responsibility of getting things accomplished at home, hire others to do some of the work, or delegate tasks to those living with you. Free up some of your valuable time so you can take that exercise class or college course you've been interested in. Your mental outlook will soar as you treat yourself to more of the delights of living—and less of the drudgery.

11. HAVE FAITH, NOT FEAR

One of the benefits of practicing inner contemplation on a regular basis is the development of a sense of faith that the universe is a warm and caring place, not a cold, impersonal one.

Faith originates from the belief that ultimately, all things work together for good. Fear stems from the conviction that events occur by chance, and thus, you are at the mercy of a random universe. Fear is essentially the belief in a negative outcome. As a basic human emotion, fear has its place—its role is to protect you from making wrong choices by sending up a red flag to get your attention; however, fear should not be a motivating factor in making career decisions or changes.

Having faith that there is an actual life plan for you can be very freeing. Knowing that events happen for a reason will direct you to be more watchful for meaningful coincidences and other helpful messages from your Soul Web network of friends, family, and acquaintances.

Of course, just because all things happen for a reason does not mean that events won't occur that can shake the very foundations of your faith, such as a layoff, termination, or some other personal trauma. If you are faced with a tough situation, put your fears out of your mind, and go about your business. You may never know why you are presented with challenges, but when those challenges come, you'll be ready with faith, not fear.

An example of handling change with optimism is the Winter individual who, with pink slip in hand, takes the tack that there's a new opportunity up ahead. Hal Lancaster, career columnist for the *Wall Street Journal*, said, "Getting fired is just another way of saying that you had the wrong job in the first place." Maintaining an upbeat attitude when it might seem easier to give up will keep you focused on the better job that is in your future.

Having faith in your own ability to make your career dreams happen is important as well. You can learn from Theodore Roosevelt, the former President of the United States known for tenacity in his endeavors. He believed that individuals who strive for achievement show great courage. He said, "Whenever you are asked if you can do a job, tell 'em, 'Certainly I can!'—and get busy and find out how to do it." Take a cue from Teddy Roosevelt and keep plugging away at your career objectives—persistence and faith make a powerful combination.

12. KEEP LAUGHING!

Life seems to have a way of keeping us serious. As children, we laugh easily due to the novelty of events and our lack of responsibility. As we age and become more bogged down with duties, though, life may begin to seem mundane or even predictable. If we don't take care, we can lose our sense of playfulness, especially those of us who choose a line of work that does not bring us joy.

Laughter is good medicine for an ailing spirit. A daily dose of hilarity will go a long way toward keeping your attitude positive. Even in the midst of life and career challenges, there is something that you can find to make you smile. Watching comedies, reading amusing books, and associating with lighthearted people can work wonders.

You might as well laugh. No matter how difficult your circumstances, you can count on one thing—conditions have a way of changing.

13. THINK OF OTHERS

In your career, you have the opportunity to serve a large number of individuals. Should you choose to use your professional time just to get ahead, without providing your services from the heart, you probably will not gain the fulfillment you seek.

Your clients and superiors will appreciate the fact that you go the extra mile on your job. Practicing ethical behavior will be crucial to your ultimate job success and happiness. Whether you are a construction worker, a veterinarian, or an executive, doing your best in a heartfelt way never goes out of style.

In addition to helping others in your work life, you may want to spend some time providing volunteer or mentoring services in your off hours. If your schedule allows for such activity, you will gain a feeling of satisfaction from the act of enriching your community.

14. BE A ROLE MODEL

Being a role model for others is a big responsibility. While some people wear this mantle comfortably, others may use it as a way to promote themselves and their ideas in unwelcome ways. Remember that you have engineered yourself into this spot, so it will behoove you to comport yourself well.

To stay positive while setting a good example for others, you may need to remind yourself to wield your power responsibly. Taking the high road will guarantee that you have nothing to regret.

Just as a child will mimic the behavior of a parent, other individuals will watch your actions and perhaps even imitate them. Just because you might not see the effect you have on others does not mean you have no effect. The truth is that people tend to do what others do. Armed with that knowledge, you can go about your business knowing that your appearance, speech, and behavior will be scrutinized and emulated by those with whom you associate. Thus, becoming a positive role model helps not only you, but also everyone else who looks to you for inspiration and leadership.

15. REMEMBER EVERY DAY IS A GOOD DAY

No day is really a bad one. Your worst days can seem like nightmares, but they are certainly, in the main, learning experiences for your growth. Whether you're facing a surprise job change, a high-stress work issue, or some other career challenge, mastering your reaction to events is critical in maintaining your upbeat attitude. Though easier said than done at times, keeping your head when all around you is collapsing can be a result of your own high level of inner growth and personal strength.

That is not to say you won't ever experience episodes of sorrow where you will need to withdraw and heal, such as when you suffer a job loss or lose a coveted promotion. Being human involves intense emotion as part of the package. Because your feelings are the overriding factor in determining your own happiness, you need to pay close attention to them. It's not wise to try to shut your feelings off like a faucet if they don't seem to suit your conscious thoughts. For this reason, the more important task is to sustain your inner balance—a place of calm from which you can derive great comfort and joy.

WHY SHOULD I WORK AT STAYING POSITIVE?

In a world of increased technology, instant communication, and greater-than-ever impersonalization, people often find themselves groping for ways to recover the joy that's missing from their lives and careers. On the road, the faces of passersby reflect their tension, fatigue, and general malaise. Perhaps you feel down more often than you would prefer.

We're constantly bombarded with negative news stories that stimulate our emotions. In fact, we sometimes get the impression that not much good takes place in our world. The result of paying attention to only the depressing events of life can be a downcast and hopeless attitude. We begin to believe that the world has virtually no redeeming features.

One important reason to remain optimistic is that you will attract more career opportunities. If you are an upbeat person, you will pull more positive people and events to you, because you are open to them. So, in a very practical sense, maintaining a joyful attitude will reward you by making your path to success easier.

Another reason to stay positive is to add more light to your individual world. Enthusiasm is contagious, and your optimistic outlook will help others in your circle to see that there's a better way to handle life and career situations. In addition, when you have the occasion to interact with strangers or clients, you'll be able to brighten their days with your own cheerful point of view. A smile and a kind comment can be your pebble dropped into the ocean of life—watch as it ripples in ways you couldn't have imagined.

6

SPRING
YOUR SEASON OF NEW GROWTH

In my hut this spring, there is nothing—there is everything!
—Eden Phillpotts

Spring, the beginning of the career season cycle, is a time for planting seeds and for laying the groundwork of future career success. No matter what your age, Spring means you're making a new start, accompanied by all the excitement and wonder of a child who has a whole lifetime ahead. Whether you're eighteen or sixty, Spring marks a busy period where you will select a profession and begin the climb to job competence and eventually, if all goes well, to your season in the sun.

Like a bud getting ready to ripen, you are beginning a road of progress in a new field of interest. You might have retired from, or ended, another vocation recently, and you're taking the first steps in a career that fascinates you. Perhaps your entire life has been spent dreaming of the day you could begin this very career venture, and now your vision has become real.

Then again, you might be fresh out of school or entering the workforce for the first time after raising a family, and testing out your first occupation. The prospect fills you with anticipation. Not certain if your career will match its potential, you look ahead to the experience and practical knowledge you'll gain from actually performing the work. At this point, keeping an open mind with few expectations will be helpful as you sail the waters of your first career.

No matter how you find yourself in the Spring season, you'll have the opportunity to see if your chosen career is all you dreamed it could be. If it doesn't pan out for you, you'll be able to make adjustments as you go, by paying attention to your inner wisdom.

As in nature, there are early, middle, and late phases of Spring. There is no timetable for you to determine how long the individual stages of your Spring may last. Depending on the career you choose, your own motivation for success, and other personal factors, your Spring could be relatively short or quite drawn out.

EARLY SPRING

This first stage of Spring marks a period where you are an explorer seeking new employment lands. Untapped territory is before you, and a feeling of adventure is in the air. Now's your time to narrow the field of job choices and make your first moves toward that ideal career. You might find yourself in one of these early Spring circumstances.

- You just graduated from high school or college.

- You accepted your first job.

- You're researching possible career options.

- You're starting your own business.

- You're starting to work outside the home after being a full-time homemaker.

- You're returning to the workforce after a period of unemployment.

- You retired from one job and you've just started a new career.

- You're retraining for another career because you can no longer perform your old job.

- You've begun a new position after quitting a job.

THE GRADUATE

Fresh out of high school, college, or a training program, you're ready to enter your field. Now you'll be expected to play the interview game—with the requisite thirty-second commercial when asked to "tell me about yourself." Before you get to the interview, you should be fully prepared to discuss yourself, your qualifications, and what makes you right for the job. To get a job in the field you love, your education, experience, and skills have to be right on the tip of your tongue.

If your previous work experience in your field is minimal, you'll want to highlight your education on your résumé and focus on your potential during job interviews. Any work experience you do have should show that you're able to take direction and work as a member of a team. Remember, everyone has to start somewhere, so a lack of experience should not be a hindrance to following your career dreams.

Your First Job

You've done your research and passed the interview process with flying colors, and now you have your first job. You are now poised to launch what may turn out to be your path of service. You have something to prove now—to yourself and to others in your profession. Do you have what it takes to make it in your chosen field, and can this career sustain your interest over the long haul?

You can use the time in your first job wisely by making sure to go the extra mile for your boss even when you are not asked to do so. Initiative and hard work tend to be recognized and rewarded and a little extra effort could result in higher company profits and personal advancement. In addition, exhibiting integrity at all times will assure that you're considered a solid member of the company team.

Entering or Returning to the Workforce

At present you may be returning to the workforce or entering the ranks of the employed for the first time, perhaps after years spent raising a family. Besides the obvious challenges of adjusting to a new work schedule, you may have another hurdle to get over—believing that you have something to contribute.

You may suppose that you have no current job skills to offer, or that you're too old to be starting over. If you have worked in a particular career field in the past, you may need to renew your skills, but you have plenty to offer from the standpoint of your maturity and desire to succeed.

If you have never held a job outside of the home, you'll want to take a closer look at those skills you may have taken for granted. You probably have an assortment of valuable skills that you can translate into a thriving career, including any committees you've participated in, groups you've coached, or household budgeting and accounting you've done. First, do a thorough self-assessment of your interests and talents. Next, choose a career goal and begin a series of action steps to make it happen.

RETIRED WITH A FRESH START

Transitioning from retirement to a new employment opportunity can occur in early middle age or in later years. You might have had a long career in one place or used a primary skill working for several employers. No matter how your career progressed, you are undergoing a major life change in early Spring.

Think back to old career dreams that might need to be reactivated. Because money may not be a big issue for you now, you probably can be more flexible in your choice of new work. Perhaps you can decide on a job that's performed purely for the joy it gives you, with a paycheck being merely the icing on the cake. All of your previous hard work has earned you the luxury of doing what you want at this time.

THE RETURNEE

You're the individual who had a long tenure in a field you really loved. You have exciting options for growth now, including using your skills as a consultant, opening your own business, or teaching others what you know. In essence, you can choose this time to continue to practice, albeit in a different capacity, in your chosen field.

Spread the word about your services. Keep in touch with people in your old office for any leads, and contact local colleges, training centers, and government agencies to find out if they have a need for your particular expertise. If you're a member of any professional associations, be sure to attend their meetings for information about potential work opportunities. With your many talents and years of experience, it won't be long until you're well on your way to the second phase of your dream career.

FINDING YOUR CAREER PATH

It seems clear that some people know what career path to take from an early age. They appear to be driven by an inner taskmaster and remain focused on their goal in every respect. On the other hand, some of us may not find that career pathway as easily, and could spend years searching for the perfect career niche. All in all, professional achievement boils down to hard work and persistence for everyone; however, there are actions you can take to begin career exploration. Here are some examples.

- Let your Soul Web network know that you're seeking employment.

- Utilize the Department of Labor's website for employment assistance (ows.doleta.gov).

- Go to your local college or university career center for testing. Take the COPS system tests (interests, abilities, and work values); Myers-Briggs Type Indicator (how your personality type best fits into certain work settings); and CHOICES (a computer-aided career assessment tool that gives you career path alternatives around interests and abilities, plus information on higher education, training, and financial aid).

- Use the Internet to research occupations and companies that employ people with your career interests.

- Review the *Occupational Outlook Handbook* (bls.gov/oco or at your local library, career center, or bookstore) for occupational trends, requirements, and typical wages.

- Research your local, state, and federal government websites and publications for information on available jobs and how to apply for them.

- Attend job fairs for current information about job openings.

- Talk with people working in your field of interest. If possible, arrange an informational interview with someone to tour the facilities and to get a feel for whether you'd like that kind of work.

- Visit your local chamber of commerce for labor market data and business contacts.

- Utilize your telephone directory's yellow pages for business names and numbers. The phone book is a great, underused resource for career seekers.

- Update your résumé at a local career center.

- Take a look at your area newspapers' want ads. Because the jobs listed are seen by thousands, the employers tend to ask for higher skills than they actually need in order to limit the pool of eligible applicants.

- Visit job-search websites on a regular basis. One excellent job database is America's Job Bank (ajb.dni.us).

- Take an adult education or extended-learning class or seminar in your area of interest.

- Volunteer some time in your field of interest. It will give you the chance to test out the career and may open pathways to paid employment.

- Turn a hobby into paying work on a part-time basis. Later on you could decide to switch to full time if it goes as well as you'd hoped it would.

- Consider staffing agencies to help you get your foot in the door of potential employers. If you prove to be a good worker, a career could be in the making.

- See a professional career counselor or coach. You could be set on the best path quickly.

- Visit a library or bookstore for information on careers and how to make career choices and changes.

- Evaluate your employment history, skills, and career dreams honestly. The more you know about yourself, the better you'll be able to make the most beneficial career decisions.

MIDSPRING

You have established yourself in a career by the middle of Spring. In general, your job choice appears to be compatible with your long-term career goals at this point. In this phase of growth, you are likely eyeing ways to advance in your chosen field. This is a period to assess how satisfied you are with your career progress while you continue to move forward on the job.

You may be experiencing some of these aspects at Midspring.

- Learning as much as you can while on the job

- Growing your business

- Feeling fairly convinced that you're in the right career

- Gaining the respect of your coworkers and boss

- Continuing to look for advancement opportunities

- Maintaining enthusiasm for the job

In this stage of Spring, you're feeling comfortable with your work environment and you tend to get along well with coworkers and superiors. You're continuing to make a name for yourself at this point, your work gives you a sense of accomplishment, and you're enthusiastic about applying your strengths to meet company goals. All in all, things are going smoothly and the seeds of the season are starting to bloom.

During Midspring, your dedication to your work begins to show. You could be moving up the growth spiral now, where you feel happy in your career and are benefiting others because of your commitment.

LEARNING ON THE JOB

In this stage of Spring, you may want to involve yourself in some special projects in order to learn more about your job and to challenge your abilities. In addition, you will want to take advantage of training opportunities to augment your skills. The more you learn, the more likely you are to become a resident expert—and soon you'll have others knocking on your door for answers.

TIME TO GROW A BUSINESS

The time-consuming early groundwork of starting your own business has begun to reap its first rewards. Energized by the positive feedback you receive from your customers and the community at large, it's becoming clear that you are establishing a brand.

If instead, however, you find that having your own business is becoming too much of a headache, you'll need to evaluate whether it is truly the right path of service for you.

If you are in need of free and confidential small business counseling, contact the Service Corps of Retired Executives (SCORE) through its website, score.org. Two heads are often better than one, and an expert opinion may help you to see alternatives you hadn't considered. To find a local chapter or to get more information, call SCORE at (800) 634-0245.

LATE SPRING

The pivotal time of late Spring may contain a fork in the road. Taking one road or the other could now set the tone for the rest of your career cycle. At this time, you are either moving confidently toward the Summer season or you are beginning to question your career choices.

This is the point of decision. If you choose to remain in your current career even though it may offer little or no fulfillment, it could become more difficult as time goes on to extricate yourself from it. Getting entrenched in a job just for the money can lead you directly past your place in the sun to Autumn.

Then again, let's suppose that you have found the career of your dreams this Spring. Although you may have found true job fulfillment, you'll want to keep learning and growing in your field.

Here are some of the facets of late Spring, which can vary widely, depending upon your feelings about your current career.

- Returning to school part-time to upgrade your skills

- Becoming frustrated and confused about where your career is headed

- Gaining more and more competence in your position

- Continuing to build your dream career

- Questioning whether you will ever be promoted at your current company

- Getting feedback that your boss, coworkers, or clients appreciate your work

RETURNING TO SCHOOL

Whether or not you are in a profession that requires you to continue your formal education or to get specific certifications or licenses to be considered for advancement, lifelong learning has taken on a new significance in most fields. It can benefit you to add to your knowledge base while going through any career season.

You may find yourself questioning whether school is the right place for you in late Spring and whether the cost, in terms of both time and money, will be worth it if the education turns out to be of negligible benefit to your career. Keep in mind that some employers offer tuition reimbursement or even free education to assist you in your upward path, which might make your decision considerably easier.

Make sure you know your employer's policy toward higher education or training. Employers differ widely on how much they'll contribute to your education, so find out the facts to make an informed decision for your future.

Career Confusion

In late Spring, you may be undergoing some major uncertainty about where your career is headed. Maybe you've done all the right things—you've volunteered for extra projects, shown up early to your job, been a team player, and been above reproach in your character—but you're not getting much satisfaction from your job.

Maybe you're not certain you want to remain in your present job at all. You're not sure you can ever move up within this company, which doesn't necessarily mean that your career is the problem—you may just be with the wrong company. Continual frustration, anger, or disappointment signal that you may need to change your circumstances before the situation becomes intolerable.

The truth is that sometimes a job will not be a good fit—no matter how you may try to force it to happen. If that's becoming the case for you, it might be time to look for a new position either within the company or elsewhere. Shaking things up by way of change often can bring fresh perspective and new energy into your life.

Rapid Rise

You could be on an upward career roll in late Spring, feeling more competent and gaining further respect from your superiors. Your enthusiasm for your work has been buoyed by the recognition that is starting to come your way. Perhaps your boss uses you for a sounding board when she has a complicated issue that needs to be resolved. She may come to you for advice even though others have been at the job far longer. You've proven your worth to the company, and now you set your sights on a well-deserved raise. Continue in this manner and you will soon be entering the Summer season of your career.

Your Own Business

If you're at the helm of your own company, late Spring can be the starting point of high growth. You've committed to staying with your business to see how far it will take you. You chose the path at the fork in the road that may lead to your place in the sun.

Rachel, a small business owner for more than two years now, says, "I had to learn a lot about running my own business in the opening year—things I didn't think about before I began. On the first anniversary of my company, I had to make a decision whether to keep my business going or to walk away. I chose to stick with it, for better or worse."

Conversely, if you determine at the crossroads that you'd be better off closing your business, you are now faced with the prospect of a whole new career enterprise. You can start over with the knowledge that you can create other, very likely better, career opportunities.

MANUEL'S CAREER PATH

A young man in the late Spring season of his career, Manuel obtained a degree in psychology from a university in his native Mexico. With a specialty in industrial psychology, he put his skills to good use after graduation when he accepted a position in the pharmaceutical industry. After falling in love with an American citizen, Manuel married and moved to the United States.

Although an intelligent and talented professional, in the United States Manuel faced a tough job market in his chosen field. He sought positions in his desired vocation but to no avail. Finally, desperate to find work, he accepted a job in the human resources department of a company.

At first the position looked bright; it offered him the opportunity to interview a variety of people, which he truly enjoyed. Some situations cropped up that led him to question the management and leadership abilities of his boss—in Mexico, he had encountered managers with remarkable people skills and leadership talents. Manuel couldn't help but make comparisons between them and this new boss.

In fact, as Manuel puts it, "In Mexico, the managers at my company were my role models. They taught me how people needed to be shown respect in order to give a business their best efforts. Now I am aware that I am a role model for others, and I act accordingly. The things I learned from them will stay with me all of my life."

Realizing that he cannot commit to his current job as his path of service, Manuel is seeking other employment. He attends school on a part-time basis to gain more job skills. With a goal of eventually returning to the pharmaceutical industry, Manuel is beginning to take steps toward that aim.

Having reached late Spring, Manuel is combining work with part-time school to prepare himself to move on to a more fulfilling field. A natural go-getter, he sets goals and makes them materialize. Manuel says, "I consider myself a success whenever I achieve one of my goals." With a positive attitude like that, it won't be long before Manuel finds his place in the sun.

As you can see, a person can remain in a career Spring indefinitely by trying out various short-term jobs. Until you commit to a particular career path, you will keep making new employment beginnings in Spring.

INNER CONTEMPLATION: THE CAREER EXPLORER

Close your eyes and relax in a comfortable position. You, like any intrepid explorer, need courage, faith, and persistence to discover new land during your Spring season. As an explorer, you can follow your charts, but you must be flexible for a change of course at a moment's notice. See yourself at the helm of your own career ship, in confident control of your voyage. Realize that you have all of the ability you need to find the way to your career destination.

Your Spring season can be a time of excitement, growth, and exploration, eventually leading to a rewarding career. You don't have to be in a hurry to choose the right profession. It's okay to try out different jobs to see if they're a good fit for you. By taking time to discover your vocational interests in the Spring season, you'll be well prepared to find the career path that suits you best.

7

SUMMER

A SEASON IN THE SUN

Our way is not soft grass, it's a mountain path with lots of rocks. But it goes upward, forward, toward the sun.
——RUTH WESTHEIMER

SUMMER IS LARGELY THE interlude when optimism prevails and success runs high. The Summer season is the period when you reach job fulfillment, or when you are well on your way to the ultimate career accomplishment.

Once you reach the career pinnacle, you may be convinced that your high flight will never end. It may not be feasible to maintain success at the top level—sooner or later, without a change in your career cycle, you could burn out like a supernova and quickly enter the Autumn of your career. Another possible challenge for you in

Summer is that you could discover that you've neglected important aspects of your life because you wanted career triumph.

Achievement requires patience and determination. There is always a trade-off in terms of what you are willing to give up to get what you want. To find your season in the sun, whether in Spring, Summer, Autumn, or Winter, you must reassess yourself and your goals at regular intervals along the way. Be aware that great ambition and success may unbalance the other areas of your life unless you take pains to compensate.

EARLY SUMMER

In early Summer, you're continuing your commitment to your career after finalizing your direction in late Spring. Beginning to reap your just rewards, you have your own special characteristics in the first phase of Summer. These may include one or more of the following.

- Getting a promotion or salary increase

- Feeling as though your work is more like play

- Reaching a higher level of job competence and knowledge

- Continuing to maintain great enthusiasm for your job

- Persisting in your career objectives

- Beginning to reap rewards from your business

Your Work Is Valued

Continuing the late Spring tendency to gain positive feedback from superiors or associates, your work has attracted more attention than ever. You are an integral part of the team; others look up to you for your creativity and productivity. The wheels of the workplace would not turn without your contribution, and everyone knows it.

When you propose your original ideas, others pay attention. This may be an excellent period for you to begin to implement helpful techniques or strategies to effect positive change in your business or profession.

Now you are continuing to build your reputation through ethical and honest behavior. You know that there's no particular rush to grab the brass ring, so you focus on doing the best job you can right now.

Beware that in your zeal to make a name for yourself you do not take career shortcuts that are not in your best interest. Shortcuts can end up causing embarrassment and even failure.

An example of an ego gone awry is the young musician who is catapulted to the top of the charts before he has learned to handle fame and fortune. Believing his own press, his choice of acting as a boor instead of as a role model or leader will affect not only his own path, but also the paths of his fans. Because successful individuals are role models for the young and old alike, it may be your duty to monitor your own behavior, especially once you attain public recognition for your achievements. The pebble tossed into the pond has enormous impact, and so do you, as you make your way to the podium of success.

YOUR WORK IS PLAY

Part of the joy of finding your perfect work is discovering that your livelihood can be fun. The best career is one that doesn't feel like work at all, one that rewards you by being interesting, creative, and profitable all at once. If you have found your authentic path of service, your profession will fit you like a glove and bring you to the highest level of fulfillment.

CHANGE OF HEART

If, in early Summer, you find that your work has ceased to be the ideal profession for you, now's the time to determine your next step.

You might have missed the path marked "Career Change" at the fork in the road in late Spring; the lure of good money and high achievement might have blinded you to the fact that your work wasn't food for your soul, just meat for your table.

It's never too late to correct your career direction. Take a hard look at what happened to lessen your interest in this field. It could be that your career still intrigues you but the workplace itself has grown stifling. If you love what you do for a living, then a change of work environment, and not a change of career, may be in order.

If it's your career that has lost its sparkle, can you regain it? You may be able to use your creativity at work by proposing a new project or an idea that can serve to boost your enthusiasm for your work. Being stuck in a rut doesn't have to last. Sometimes it's as simple as making an attitude adjustment about your job to relieve a humdrum work existence.

Maybe you need to move *up* in your career, not out. Consider additional training and/or higher education that would allow you to be promoted to a more interesting spot. To alleviate boredom and stagnation, many successful people recommend making a job change as soon as you master a position.

MIDSUMMER

As a Midsummer person, you have made significant career progress. You show up in the right place at the right time, and everything you touch seems to turn to gold. Opportunities for advancement appear to be everywhere, and your career pinnacle is at hand. You've earned it with your perseverance and dedication.

Here are some notable signposts of the Midsummer stage.

- Reaching the career pinnacle

- Feeling that your career is your calling

- Showing signs of your leadership potential

- Starting to feel the strain of a lot of work and too little personal time

- Advancing rapidly up the career ladder

- Receiving acknowledgment of your expertise on the job

- Earning the salary commensurate with your dreams

REACHING YOUR ZENITH

This is what you've dreamed of for so long—you've climbed your way to the peak of the mountain, and the view is unsurpassed. Your own particular summit may hold a prestigious award, a major contract, or an important promotion. Suddenly all your monumental efforts have paid off.

YOUR CAREER IS YOUR CALLING

In Midsummer, you've attained a spot that can allow you to exert positive influence in the world. You've become a role model, whether you intended to or not—and your every movement and statement are evaluated for consistency and character. Seeing the big picture and the value of teamwork, you can function independently on complex issues, but understand the importance of consulting with others on the team. In your world, everybody counts.

As someone with a calling, you may find yourself the leader of a few who do not share your vision or mission. There will always be people in it for their own gain, people who are not interested in creating positive change. If you are surrounded with that ilk, you can try to convince them of your views or you may need to send them on their way. Another option for you is to take the step to leave, and to find a spot that attracts like-minded individuals.

WHEN YOUR EGO TAKES CHARGE

At this point in your career, depending on your level of inner growth, your ego may be dominant or not an issue at all.

An out-of-control ego could create some unwanted effects in Midsummer, including conceit, rudeness, aggression, and greed. If left untamed, your ego will always require the latest toy or sensation to appease it.

Knowing that your ego can never be content, you have two choices. You can elect to control your ego or you can continue to let it take charge. The key here is in realizing that by letting your ego remain in control, you cannot attain complete fulfillment. Profound happiness comes from the inside, and not from satisfying material desires.

LIFE BALANCE

If you're a top achiever, striking a balance between work and personal life can be a worthy, although a challenging, goal. Before you realize what's happening, you could be putting in fourteen hours a day on the job. From your perspective, a long workday is not too much to ask in order for you to achieve your career objectives. Perhaps in your mind, all your exertion is for the greater good of you and your family.

Being focused on getting ahead is admirable, but it can lead to fallout where your family or friends are concerned. When your family or other close relations begin to voice objections about the lack of time they are able to spend with you, take heed. At this point, you may find their requests for your attention unreasonable—after all, you may feel that you're doing all of this work for *them*.

Paying attention to your personal life now will help you to avoid possible difficulties in the future, when you may be scratching your head and asking, "What happened?" Regardless of your marital status or family situation, you'll want to take a look at the existing equilibrium between your work and private life. Taking action as soon as you become aware of trouble is the solution to staying on an even keel.

KEEPING A BALANCE

Are you unable to find time to spend with your family and friends?

Review your schedule to see what activities you can cut out—too much work and no play can be counterproductive. Your close relations may become resentful of your work and its demands on your time.

Do you have free time for yourself?

Evaluate whether you have time each day for your own wants and needs. Even if you have to schedule a block of time for yourself in your daily calendar, do it—you deserve some peaceful moments just for you. You'll be able to return to work more refreshed as a result.

Are you feeling pressure from your job?

If you have too much to do at work, it could be an ongoing situation. Some jobs are inherently busy with little downtime, but that doesn't mean you have to sacrifice your personal life for your work. Maybe it's time to make some decisions about the intense demands of your career.

Is the big money worth it?

You might be working many overtime hours to keep your paychecks large. Maybe your company requires you to be available at a moment's notice and compensates you accordingly. Whatever the case, you need to consider whether a high salary is enough of a trade-off for the lack of personal time.

Are you happy?

Perhaps you are happiest when you work hard at your job. If you're content with your life even though you have a full schedule, you may not have any balance issues. But if you ever feel your balance begin to slip away, take quick action to get things back on track.

LATE SUMMER

Having reached the top of your game through hard work, you may find yourself looking out the window much more often. "What else is there?" you may find yourself asking. Have you hit the end of the road in this career? That idea may not sit well with you and could begin to erode your peace of mind. After all, you've accomplished great things already. What's next? You start to ponder a way you can climb even higher—or perhaps the next path is a different one altogether. These are some signs to watch for in late Summer:

- An internal voice asking "Where do I go from here?"

- An internal voice saying "I've reached my peak; I guess that's as good as it gets . . . "

- Considering a move to another career altogether

- Realizing you'd like to take some time off for yourself and your family

- Lessening enthusiasm for the same, albeit successful, routine

- Feeling isolated from the everyday workings of the business

- Reexamining your long-range goals

- Thinking about retooling yourself within your current career

WHAT NEXT?

The sun has reached its zenith in your career, and you've succeeded in everything you set out to accomplish. In late Summer, you could find yourself without a challenge or a new puzzle to solve. There are signs that the sun may be shining a little less brightly for you now. Where do you go from here?

Like the movie actor turned director, you may be able to move on to another facet of your field once your initial passion for your current job wears off. Remaining in the same career but in a new capacity revitalizes your workday by allowing you to learn other skills and challenge yourself to a greater degree.

THIS IS AS GOOD AS IT GETS

Maybe you've decided that there's nowhere else to go after reaching your career summit. Whatever your position, you might feel that you can't (or won't) go any higher in your profession. Content with the way your career is going, you show up to work with a smile— after all, you're well compensated for your efforts at this point in your life, and you hold a certain amount of power in your position.

There are no more dragons to fight—and that's all right with you. In your heart, you know that not many people can match your accomplishments and that you're one of a kind.

CAREER ABOUT-FACE

For you, basking in the sunshine of Summer isn't quite enough. In the end, you have to find other mountains to conquer. Sitting around catching some rays will do only for a while. After reaching your zenith in one profession, you're ready to scale the heights elsewhere.

Like the attorney who becomes a television pundit, you might be considering using your present skills in another arena. Transitioning to a new work setting in late Summer—one that requires the expertise you gained in your current livelihood—would be a natural progression for you.

There's a possibility that you want to end all ties to your current career and start completely anew in an untested field. You're used to success by now, and you're competent in the career master thinking needed to tackle a field in which you have something to prove. After all, you're an achiever, and, like a bulldozer, you let nothing stand in your way.

Taking Time Off

Relaxing a bit could be just what you need now. You've been a hard worker, and you deserve a little time off to kick back and play. Your family will surely appreciate the time you spend with them. Although you may feel indispensable to your business, it's important for you to take time out to recharge and to recreate to keep your motivation and spirits high. You can rest assured that your work will be there when you get back.

ZACHARY'S STORY

The road to success has been a long one for Zachary, and now he finds himself in the early phase of his season in the sun. An honors university graduate in business and economics, Zachary had always dreamed of a career as a financial planner, but instead took the easier route to become an accountant. Zachary admits that he let his conscious mind make his career choice, rather than allowing his inner wisdom to guide him to his path of service.

Climbing the corporate ladder led to the challenge of trying to cope with downsizing and reorganizations. All of his company's reshuffling effectively prevented him from advancing to a senior executive post. Finally, after nine years in corporate finance, Zachary took charge of his destiny and set off to become an entrepreneur.

Financial planning was Zachary's true path of service, as demonstrated by his passion for the work and a strong commitment to his clients.

Knowing that financial abundance is just around the corner, Zachary is glad he followed his heart to pursue his career dream. Zachary says, "I've hit bottom in my working life on many occasions. Each and every time this has happened, it has strengthened me even more."

Until he made the move to become a financial planner, Zachary knew full well that he was not following his path of service. "I always questioned my career as an accountant but felt too comfortable to leave. Finally, I took the plunge, took on the risk, and ventured out on my own. I believed this was my calling."

Committed to his company, he and his business partner continue to build a solid foundation in the early Summer career season. As Zachary says, "Some people are guided to figure out their passion and unique ability. I consider myself very fortunate that I've found my own path of service."

INNER CONTEMPLATION: THE DISCOVERY

As a career master of the high seas, you're in charge of your employment destination. Having discovered new land successfully in the Summer of your career, you're basking in the moment and getting ready to tackle additional horizons. Think about how far you've come on your career journeys already. Take a look back at all the steps you took toward your goals. Review all your accomplishments. After imagining where you've been, think about where you want to go. What will your future accomplishments be?

Reaching the Summer pinnacle of success can be worth every minute of your hard work and diligent preparation. Take time to congratulate yourself for your Summer achievements before jumping in to tackle your next set of goals. Don't forget to pat yourself on the back occasionally for each victory you achieve in your zeal to make it to the top of your profession.

8

AUTUMN

THE SEASON OF CHANGING COLORS

September tries its best to have us forget summer.
—BERN WILLIAMS

ON THE HEELS OF SUMMER is Autumn, a time for slowing down from the intensity of the hottest career season.

Now you are at the crossroads of your employment life. You can choose a new direction at this juncture or accept a comfortable existence in a job you've mastered.

The Autumn career season can come on gradually or by apparent surprise. If you've been in a job for a long period of time, your day-to-day activities have become second nature by now. Then one day you wake up and realize you're bored—the Autumn season has arrived. On the other hand, there might come a rapid shift in the form of a company reorganization. If that happens, any opportunity for advancement may dry up. Then again, you could be getting tired of the particular demands of your position, and a busy day of unrewarding tasks may not suit you any longer. No matter how you enter the Autumn season, you are now facing a possible change of direction.

It's at this point that you need to get a clear picture of your commitment to your career by assessing what has changed—perhaps the reasons you chose this career in the first place are no longer viable; it's entirely possible that you have outgrown your work.

Like wearing a tight pair of shoes that should have been replaced long ago, your career path may need to be expanded to fit your developing needs. To remain in a dissatisfying job will only increase your feelings of tension and disappointment.

Instead of accepting decline as a natural part of life and of your career, see your Autumn season as a wakeup call for you to take action.

A NATURAL PROGRESSION

Should you choose to remain in your profession even though it may have lost a bit of its luster, you could be following a natural progression of the career cycle leading to the onset of Winter. If you decide not to pursue any new vocational course and wait until your Winter retirement, that is your alternative. Your working life is your own—to plan, to fulfill, and to end—as your heart leads you.

Sometimes a job is not challenging anymore but still has elements that contribute to your wish to remain. Perhaps your work affords you the valuable benefit of a social outlet, or maybe you have the freedom to work at your own pace with little supervision. Your job could be relatively relaxed, and you might not be able to find another position with the same great perks—so you stay. There are a million reasons why you should keep your present occupation, but how much do they really matter if your job does not fulfill your career needs and wants?

Autumn can be an exciting time. It can be a period of setting new goals to enliven a sagging career. Because you possess valuable job skills and knowledge, you have options for movement and growth.

EARLY AUTUMN

The first phase of the Autumn career season may sneak up on you undetected.

How could this have happened? You've managed to pass through the hot success of Summer only to find yourself suddenly treading water in Autumn. The good news is that there is plenty of time to change from career stagnation to fulfillment once again. Watch for these key signs in early Autumn.

- Increasing lack of interest and enthusiasm for your job

- Having no new career goals

- Considering learning new skills to advance or to change jobs

- Feeling comfortable, though blasé

- Beginning to gain weight due to boredom

- Performing your job robotically

LOSING INTEREST

In early Autumn it's becoming apparent that your job enthusiasm has dropped a notch or two. The ennui has grown, and you're not sure you can refuel your fervor for another go-round.

Perhaps the daily commute is becoming hard to take—you might feel as though you're driving to an unwanted destination. More and more, you seem to be playacting your way through the job. Your heart may not be in your livelihood, but your mind keeps reminding you that you need the money and security of it. Still, there are a few glimmers of joy to be found at work. It's not all a bed of thorns—yet.

NONEXISTENT CAREER GOALS

Maybe it's been a long time since you've set a career goal for yourself, or you've never pursued a goal at all—you simply might have fallen into an occupation. In early Autumn, your list of career objectives is blank—there's nowhere to go and nothing for which to strive. Perhaps there's little opportunity for upward mobility in your business, so you've settled in for a long stay at your current position.

You might be the public defender with years of experience representing the downtrodden. Once upon a time, you were passionate about your job, but now you're beginning to see your clients as indistinguishable from one another—they seem to have the same issues and attitudes. Now's a good time to take out the career mirror and examine the visage you see. What continues to hold you to your post? Is it the security of your salary, or the chance you have to make a difference?

It's not too late to create some new employment goals, which doesn't mean you need to change careers; perhaps it's as simple as examining where you find fulfillment in your current position and how you can increase the experience of job satisfaction.

MAKING YOUR OWN OPPORTUNITY

Now you could be thinking about rekindling the flames of employment passion. Perhaps you're looking at going back to school so that you can move ahead in your company or to aid yourself in making a total career change. In early Autumn, you toss ideas for growth around in your mind but generally take no action on them. You might tell your coworkers about your plans to continue your education, but you're not quite ready to take a big step.

For years, Dennis has insisted that he wants to go back to school for his advanced degree—but nothing's happened yet. Had he returned to the university when he first considered it, he would have finished his education by now. At this point in his career, it would be easier for Dennis to float along until retirement, instead of putting out the extra energy it would take to complete his studies. Do not be like Dennis and let inaction deter you from achieving your goals.

MIDAUTUMN

If you have allowed the ennui of early Autumn to build without a challenge, you may find yourself becoming more acclimated to a work life of drifting. Perhaps on automatic pilot during this phase, you haven't quite gotten the message that you might have to take charge of your destiny soon—if you don't, your career will remain in limbo. At this stage, you could be missing your cues for career progress. Here are some of the earmarks that may accompany Midautumn.

- Coasting through the workweek

- Getting tired of seeing the same faces at work each day

- Suffering from low energy

- Spending more time on personal phone calls at the office

- Withdrawing from interaction with coworkers

- Difficulty pretending that you care about your job

COASTING THROUGH THE JOB

Low energy can dog you in the Midautumn phase of your career cycle. Although you don't know it yet, your heart has decided that this work isn't your true path of service. Through your feelings, your career master is trying to show you that there's something better for you out there.

Your workweek goes by slowly, and the monotony of the job drains you more and more. At work, you fill your time with personal phone calls and other matters that would be better suited for home— you pay your bills, balance your checkbook, and read the morning newspaper at your desk.

The best part of the day is lunch. For you, this means a respite from the reality of your circumstances. Your "real world" is outside of those work walls.

Tired of seeing the same old faces with their tense expressions and limited concerns, you start to avoid any interaction with your coworkers. You tell yourself it's better this way because they only want to discuss work issues and you have no interest in talking about the job anymore.

CAREER LIMBO

You've reached a point of career limbo. Until your work situation gets bad enough for you to take notice, you will remain in a dream world where you fool yourself into thinking that everything's quite all right. Now is the time to look for an authentic reflection in your career mirror.

Terry showed up for work each day with a frown that he didn't know he was wearing. In his mind, work was not supposed to be joyful; it was just a way to pay his mortgage and other financial obligations. Toiling in a hectic nonprofit agency, Terry was unfulfilled but completely oblivious to it. Eventually, Terry woke up to his career reality and moved on to a more satisfying position in a different field. Now his image in the career mirror is an authentic one.

LATE AUTUMN

"Am I really happy doing what I'm doing?" This is the question you may ask yourself as you enter the late Autumn phase. You may need to find a reason to take action to enliven your career. Perhaps being bored is not enough to spur you on to change. Only you can decide if a lack of job fulfillment is enough to motivate you to swim out of the depths of career tedium.

Late Autumn may present some of these contrasting characteristics, depending upon your level of inner growth and your current choices.

- Becoming aware of fulfillment needs

- Attempting to renew career motivation by changing your outlook

- Deciding to return to school to learn new skills

- Considering a lateral job transfer to infuse new excitement

- Vacillating between making a career move or staying put

- Resigning yourself to a dull work life until it's time to retire

- Risking superiors noticing that your work is slacking off

- Taking more time away from your job

- Setting new career goals

BECOMING AWARE OF THE DILEMMA

In late Autumn, you realize that you're sitting in the middle of a dilemma. Now that you know where you stand, you have several options. Do you stay in the comfort zone of the same job until retirement, knowing full well that there's little fulfillment in it? Do you decide to make new career goals for yourself? Or do you choose to waver between the two—in effect, deciding not to decide at all?

Choosing to Remain

You've thought about what it would take for you to begin again in a new field, and you're not up for it. For you, any extra effort at this point in your life is simply a waste of time and energy. You select the path of least resistance—from your perspective, the time for any advancement or a new outlook on your career has long passed. Besides, retirement isn't that far away—you can hang on for a few more years, can't you?

As you've decided to stay in your present work, you could choose to renew your motivation for the job. Because practicing positive and productive career thinking is crucial for fulfillment in any occupation, you should take charge of your thoughts and strategize about ways in which you can infuse new life and enjoyment into your work. Why not enjoy the years you have left in this profession by maintaining a positive attitude about it? At the end of the day, it's up to you.

Returning to School

Another way to make your workday more enjoyable is to pursue new skills through additional education. You may see your peers completing their advanced degrees or certificates, and thus moving up or out of the business. You have more experience than a lot of your coworkers, but it doesn't seem to count for much now.

Maybe you're feeling resentful that others are moving forward while you're still sitting down. Part of a plan to retool yourself in late Autumn could include setting some new career goals. A return to school, even on a part-time basis, might be an element of that plan. You could research scholarships, grants, and loans for the best way to finance your education and check with your employer to see how much the company would be willing to put toward your schooling.

Considering a Job Transfer

As a way to put more Spring in your step, you may be getting ready to change jobs in the same career field. Instead of taking the plunge to an entirely new profession, you've decided to renew yourself at another position in your current occupation. You feel a change of scenery will do you good at this point in late Autumn. A different job can help you to gain a revitalized outlook, which is exactly what you may need now.

Before you make that switch to a new position, make sure it's one you really want. If you find that you can't tolerate your present work anymore, you could be rushing from the frying pan to the fire in this latest spot.

Can't Make Up Your Mind

It's not uncommon to waver between making a career move and staying put in late Autumn. You could remain in a place of indecision for a long time, due to fears of losing your financial security and relative comfort should you choose to leave. You may view stepping out of a long-standing job as a huge risk instead of as an opportunity to recharge yourself.

To make any kind of career decision at this point, you may want to consult a career coach to receive immediate feedback and helpful professional guidance. Here are some typical concerns for those Autumn people who are contemplating career change.

What can I do to lessen my career boredom? I'm not quite ready to leave my job for a new career.

Choose an avocation or hobby that brings you pleasure. Doing something you enjoy may lead to a second career. If it doesn't, at least you'll be involved in a happy pastime that will add hours of joy to your life.

I'm out of practice when it comes to setting and achieving a professional goal. How do I start?

Set a goal regarding your job. Your goal could be as simple as striving to stay positive each day and to accomplish tasks with a smile. Perhaps your objective is to move to another position in your field that offers some variety. Your goal could be to plan for retirement within a specific time frame. Whatever the goal you set for yourself, focus on it and take action steps to make it happen.

My job leaves me drained at the end of the day because I'm not happy in it. Right now, career change is out of the question for me.

Take a class in something just for the fun of it. You'll meet other people with similar interests, which could lead to new and stimulating friendships. If your private life is joyful, it will spill over into your working hours.

Sometimes I don't feel like being productive at work. I can't seem to get motivated.

Maintain a standard of excellence on the job. You owe it to yourself and your company to put forth your best efforts. If you leave your present job, you probably will want a letter of recommendation, so it behooves you to be an excellent employee. If you decide to stay in your current position, you'll need to be a hard worker and a person of integrity—your boss deserves no less from you.

How can I make a job change without completely changing careers?

Keep your eyes open for transfer options within your organization. If you're in a small company, sharing any innovative ideas that you might have could lead to a special project or a job slot created just for you. If there doesn't seem to be any opportunity for growth in your current organization, it may be time to put some feelers out at similar companies.

My attitude at work is not the best right now.

Although you may have strong opinions about your company and its management, avoid making any negative comments about your job. Word travels fast in a work environment, and any gossip attributed to you may have a powerful impact on your office reputation. Study the tips in this book for keeping your outlook upbeat. Having an optimistic attitude is a distinct advantage when it comes to making career opportunities or transitions.

I'm too nervous about the future right now to make a drastic career change.

You always have the option of changing your mind down the road if your current career doesn't work out. Review your feelings of career satisfaction every so often to see where you stand.

I'm not sure I want to go back to school to get ahead in my current career.

Going back to school just to add more letters after your name may not be what you need now. If you wish to remain in your present career, further education will help considerably by opening up your options. On the other hand, if you're looking to change careers altogether, you may or may not need more training or education right away. Make up your mind about your career path first before you take the plunge into school. Once you determine your dream career field, you'll be able to research and to plan an educational track.

I feel like quitting my job on the spot every time I come to work.

Carefully consider your options now. A rash move to quit prematurely is a common event—and not a recommended one. Your feelings are telling you that you need to make plans to move on, so act accordingly.

My job search skills are very rusty.

Consult a career coach for help with modern job-search techniques, or research job-search trends for yourself via the Internet, libraries, and bookstores. Visit a local career center for help with your résumé and to view current job leads.

I'm afraid to go out looking for work at my age.

The good news is that employers will be utilizing mature workers more than ever in the years to come. That said, it's important for you to keep your skills updated to give yourself the best possible advantage in the changing job market. A mature worker with outdated skills may have a more difficult time seeking new work.

I've decided that I'm ready to make a career change. What next?

Research—and then more research! Before you take a step, know where you're headed and what it'll take to get there. Career changes are best made with inner wisdom, smart planning, and prudent action. As a career master, be confident that you have what it takes to succeed.

MAKING THE MOST OF THE AUTUMN YEARS

If Autumn is your current season, you are in a position to renew your work motivation. Choosing to retool your work life may mean that, to find a balance, you'll be putting out more energy and possibly cutting back in other areas of your life. Now you have the choice to hide your light under a bushel—or to make new advances in a career that might have been stagnant for a long while.

As a mature Autumn person, you may believe that you have more to risk than a younger Autumn traveler. Depending on how long you've been on the Autumn road, it may appear as if there are no other options open to you other than to ride it out. But, taking a more positive outlook, it could be just the occasion for you to activate new career dreams and make them a reality.

The youthful Autumn individual may seem to have less to lose by shifting gears at this career juncture. Perhaps you're in a job that once shined brightly but now has lost its sheen, and you find yourself slogging through each week anticipating day's end and the weekend's recreation. You may feel that it's far too early in life to resign yourself to an uneventful job. If you act on that intuition for change sooner rather than later, the window of opportunity will be wide open and you can climb through. Wait too long and you may miss your chance to find the niche you're seeking until the window opens once again. Act on your inner wisdom's guidance; otherwise you may find yourself in the same boat as the older Autumn worker, bemoaning the passing of valuable career years because you did nothing to change things.

LINDA'S CAREER PATH

A mature woman with an energetic spirit, Linda was not one to make career plans at first. Married young, Linda raised several children as a stay-at-home mom. Years later when trouble brewed in her marriage she courageously walked out the door to a new life—with virtually no job experience.

Now that she needed to make a living, Linda rose to the challenge. Her first major career field was human resources. Linda loved being able to help people change their lives for the better, and she relished seeing the immediate results of her efforts. She returned to school to obtain her master's degree in personnel administration during her Spring season as well.

At that period in her life, Linda decided that she wanted to make as much money as she could, so she set her sights on becoming a general manager in the hospitality industry. By learning as much as she could about both the sales and operations sides of the hotel where she worked, she became a general manager in three years—quite an extraordinary accomplishment. Now riding high in her Summer season, Linda was making the kind of money she had dreamed of.

But she didn't have much time to enjoy it. Her Autumn season was approaching, and fast. The hotel industry began to lose its excitement for her, and Linda was worn out by the need to serve so many masters. It dawned on her that the great money she was earning was not worth the toll it was taking on her personal life—indeed, she had no personal life to speak of. Deep in her Autumn season by now, Linda had to decide what to do.

Because she knew that she didn't want to remain in a position just for the salary, she let her heart's wisdom be her guide. She left her high-paying job in order to have a balanced life. Linda says, "No longer do I need to be the big cheese. I learned that I am not my title."

At present, Linda has taken new work as a secretary. She does not have to manage people, produce a budget, or take on great responsibility. She sets other career goals for herself these days; one of her aspirations is to write a children's book. Always an optimist, Linda believes there is an answer for every problem—if one is willing to entertain unusual solutions. She uses her heart's wisdom to help her make career choices, and so far hasn't been disappointed with the results.

INNER CONTEMPLATION: THE RIVER RAFT

Relax and get into your usual comfortable position with your eyes closed. See a river in your mind's eye, and notice a small raft in the water, waiting for you to board it. Step onto the raft, and direct it to start down the river. As it flows through the water, it has two possible directions to travel on the river—the north fork or the south fork. Assign the north fork one of your possible career choices (such as changing to another career, staying in your field, and so on) and make the south fork your other choice.

Now ride the raft down the north fork, which represents your first possible career destination. How does it feel? Is the journey down the north fork pleasant, and does it fill you with joy? Is the water misting your face as you go? Are there any rapids? Note your feelings.

Next, take the raft down the south fork of the river. This fork signifies your other career option. Does this trip seem more enjoyable than the north-fork journey—or less? Notice the view as you experience the cool water splashing on your skin. Is this a peaceful journey for you or a rough one? Pay attention to your sensations.

Slowly open your eyes, and compare notes on the feelings you had as you traveled the two forks. If you do this exercise carefully, afterward you'll have a good idea which career decision to make. The River Raft contemplation can be used when you need to make an important choice of any kind.

The Autumn season is a pivotal period for any worker. Whether you decide to start fresh in a new career or stay in your present one in the Autumn season, keep your work from declining into a monotonous enterprise. If you decide to remain in your current position even though it offers you little in the way of fulfillment, there are ways to energize your life outside of your work environment. As always, the choice for growth and change is firmly in your hands.

9

WINTER

A JOURNEY THROUGH
THE SNOWY SEASON

In the depths of winter I finally learned there was in me an invincible summer.

—Albert Camus

THERE ARE TIMES IN YOUR life when you reach a place of transformation—when one career door closes and locks for good. At crossroads like these, it's easy for you to see the closed door— but, as Helen Keller stated, "Often we look so long at the closed door that we do not see the one which has opened for us." Winter marks a positive period of change that can lead to the opening of a new career door, as long as your eyes are alert to every possibility.

Goals have a way of transforming when you least expect it, and you should be prepared to make continual adjustments in your career plans as needed.

If you are now in the Winter of your career, you are faced with challenge + opportunity. The other side of the coin is Spring, which represents opportunity + challenge. It is up to you to decide which season is in your best interest, and, ultimately, it is up to you to take steps to allow for the shift of seasons.

You always have the choice to take action for change or to struggle against a circumstance that you'd rather not face—that is your freedom and your responsibility. Once you make up your mind to pursue a new employment direction, you will have begun the transition into your next career season. Taking positive action will be your mode of launching into the season of new beginnings, Spring.

BE WATCHFUL

It can be difficult to accept circumstances that appear to happen out of the blue, but inherent in every challenging condition is a lesson for you to learn.

As a rule, finding yourself in a perplexing situation doesn't come about by accident. Along the way, there were probably signs that were nudging you to be aware and to take action accordingly. It's very similar to the notion of keeping your car maintained rather than overlooking the little creaks and misalignments that hint for your attention. If you ignore the symptoms too long, you may find yourself broken down one day on the side of the road.

Winter can make its appearance with subtle warning. You could be in the warmth of the sun in the morning and face a brisk wind and clouds by lunchtime. Sometimes there may be a window to view the coming changes, but without paying attention to your inner guidance, you're apt to see just what you want to see. In that case, you might feel blindsided by events because you received no obvious warning at all.

A flagging career generally taps you on the shoulder at first. Being out of step creates a feeling of dissonance. If that feeling is ignored, the tapping becomes more frequent and insistent. This nudging may become a normal part of your Winter landscape, as day by day you become accustomed to something that continues to peck at you.

Recall that Winter, like any other career season, is not predictable in depth or duration. Winter is different for everyone, but there are common characteristics as you go through your season of frost. The length of your personal Winter is always up to you. Simply by choosing to take action, you can move on to a bright beginning in Spring.

EARLY WINTER

There are many hints that you may have reached the first stage of Winter. These early signs are distinguishable from those of late Autumn by a clear change of heart: You are no longer in Autumn's dreariness, but may have crossed into the Winter realm of discontent.

It could be that, as part of a natural cycle of change, you've made an enormous career swing by now. If so, discontent may not be your defining emotion at all. By following the wisdom of your heart, you might have circumvented any possible dissatisfaction by making a move at the right time. An example of a natural career transition is leaving your job to start a family—a major decision that is probably a happy one as well. The key characteristic of the Winter season is an event, joyful or otherwise, that signals an end to your present career cycle. You might observe these indications in early Winter.

- Disintegrating attitude

- Limited possibility for advancement

- Leaving your job to go back to school full time

- Leaving your job to start a family

- Discussion within the company about possible layoffs

- Increasing focus on retirement or quitting

YOUR ATTITUDE IS SHOWING

In early Winter, you've reached a place where there is nowhere to hide. Your feelings are out in the open, and they indicate clearly that you are unhappy in your job. You find yourself grumbling to coworkers on a regular basis about how lousy your situation is, yet you take no action to improve it.

By paying attention to your own feelings at this point, you can nip your negative behavior in the bud. You've had plenty of clues already about the need to make a career change, but you haven't listened up until now. It's never too late to follow your inner guidance—it can lead you to your path of service in a new Spring season. If you find the following thoughts ring true, it may be time for a change.

This job is really getting to me.

Examine what aspects of your work are bothering you: interpersonal, tasks, hours, salary, or level of responsibility. Can the problem areas be addressed and fixed?

I'm not sure about my next step.

First, you may want to step away from your job by taking a vacation. By removing yourself from the work environment for a while, you could gain new perspective and insights about how to handle your situation.

Maybe it's not the job—maybe the problem is with me.

Do you normally have an upbeat attitude? Do people generally find you positive and cheerful? If so, your job could very well be the culprit here. Work should be satisfying and productive, not a torturous endeavor. If your attitude is starting to turn negative due to a poor job fit, take appropriate action before you get used to a mode of pessimism.

I'm hesitant to change jobs in this economy, even though I'm not happy in my present work.

You always have a choice about your career direction. Although some periods are indeed better than others in which to make career transitions, waiting for a future "perfect time" that may never come could cause you to lose years of rewarding work in a different occupation. The answer is to research your field of interest for labor market data, educational requirements, and salary potential. To make a beneficial career decision, arm yourself with the facts. It never hurts to listen to your feelings, either—sometimes the message is loud and clear that it's the right moment to move on.

Advancement Is Limited

Maybe you feel that your upward mobility is limited because your reputation has lost its sheen or because your company is so small that there's little room for growth. Whatever the reason, if doors to advancement will not swing open for you at your current workplace, perhaps it's time to look for another place to hang your hat.

It's not too late to make changes in the way you perform your work. Examine yourself in the career mirror and make any necessary adjustments to your attitude and job productivity. You may want to begin a job search in your spare time—see what's available out there in your field, or in other professions that match your skills.

EXITING FOR SCHOOL

Whether you're at the end of an extended career ride or relatively new in your career, you might conclude in early Winter that it's time to return to school. Your job hasn't brought you quite the satisfaction you'd hoped, and the idea of further education at this point is exciting and revitalizing. By upgrading your skills, you could position yourself for a more rewarding spot in another job capacity in the same career, or move onward to an entirely different occupation.

Say, for example, that your passion is to teach music. You have been involved in the performing arts for years, although your main career has been in accounting. You believe that your path of service is to pass on your knowledge and love of music. To do this, you may need to spend some time fulfilling the specific teaching-certification requirements.

Assuming that you have come to this decision by way of intuitive messages and practical career exploration, you are embarking on a path that will garner you greater success once your period of preparation is over. Regardless of how long your training takes or how old you are at the time of your return to school, at the end of the road shines the light of new career opportunity. By following your inner wisdom, you're taking the correct action at the most auspicious time.

LEAVING TO START A FAMILY

You've been working in a field that might have been rewarding in its own way, but as part of a natural cycle of life and work, you decide to quit to begin raising a family. Perhaps one day you'll return to the same career, but you feel that now is a time for your personal life to take precedence. You are ready to devote your energies to kids and home on a full-time basis. You've made the choice to postpone or end any career plans in early Winter—when or if you make up your mind to come back into the workforce, you'll be in the Spring of your career.

While you are parenting on a full-time basis, you can pursue an avocation that could become a career later on. If, after looking to the future, you have plans to enter a career that requires more training or education, you may want to take classes at a slow but steady pace. By the time you're ready to return to work, you'll have the necessary steps accomplished already.

MIDWINTER

If you've ignored the early warning system of the first phase of Winter, you are now rapidly cascading into the rapids of Midwinter, where you could find yourself stranded on the rocks if you don't start picking up the clues. Take steps to avoid falling into late Winter, which could be the next stop on your career journey.

Take a look at what might happen to you in Midwinter.

- You're becoming increasingly stressed.

- Your business is losing money and you don't know how to turn it around.

- Your attitude is more resigned to giving up.

- You are paying less and less attention to the details of your job.

- Your supervisor is monitoring your work and your absences.

- You need a job change but you're not sure how to make it happen.

FEELING STRESSED

In Midwinter, your stress level can reach new heights. Whether you're under fire at work for slacking off or you're feeling the pressure of your own business woes, you know you need to do some-thing soon. The trick is to listen to your heart's wisdom for help with your next move and take action to reduce the stress in your life through exercise and meditation. Alternatively, you must learn how to become more productive at work and/or how to leave work at the office.

Now may be the time to consult with a career coach or other employment professional for help in moving forward with your career plans. At this juncture, you should take some practical action steps to ease your work tension and to extricate yourself from any current job dilemma. Review "Handle the Stress of Change" in Chapter 5 for more tips on easing career pressures.

FAILING AT BUSINESS

If you run your own business, your life is wrapped around its con-cerns, profits, and losses. In Midwinter, you may find that sales are slow and your profits are falling. In spite of your best efforts your hold on success seems to be slipping.

In addition to the usual factors a business owner would consider to ramp up sales, perhaps there's another issue involved—you. There's a possibility that you are simply worn out by the constant pressure of trying to make your business work.

It may be the time to ask yourself whether you're running your business or vice versa. Perhaps your heart's wisdom is urging you now to retool, retire, or research a new pathway to fulfillment. For small business assistance and to explore your options, visit these Internet sites: score.org and sba.gov.

MAKING YOUR JOB CHANGE HAPPEN

You need a career adjustment, but you don't know how to make it happen. Acting too hastily will not help you—grabbing another position just because it's available may send you down a career detour. Now is the time to carefully consider how you should break out of your Winter season.

Finding out what success means to you can be a good start on the road to increased self-awareness. Taking a hard look at what has held you in your current job can be a revelation. Once you understand why you've stayed in your particular position for as long as you have, you'll be better equipped to determine what it will require to choose the path of professional achievement and fulfillment at the next fork in the road.

LATE WINTER

The last part of Winter is a time you can use to your advantage. There is no better way to refresh your life than to leave circumstances that don't benefit you for new avenues of opportunity.

With a positive attitude and the desire to take action, your Winter experience is likely to develop quickly into Spring, at which point you'll be able to prepare for your next job move with optimism and confidence.

See if you find yourself in some of these typical late Winter signs.

- You are about to lose your job or have been terminated.

- You may require time off to regain your balance or health.

- You close the doors to your business.

- You quit your long-standing job.

- You're suffering the consequences of taking career shortcuts.

- You have challenges with job retention over a long period of time.

Job's Over

It's time to face facts—you're out of a job. Whether by layoff, termination, or downsizing, you are now free to begin again. Maybe you've closed the doors to your business for the last time and don't know what to do next. You might have given your notice to quit, realizing there must be greener pastures out there for you. The good news is that once you are out of work, a whole world of new opportunities opens up.

In late Winter, you've reached the end of a career cycle, which means that a brand-new cycle can begin.

Taking Care of Yourself

At this stage you might be in the grip of a serious physical or mental health issue that requires your full attention. Perhaps you'll have to take a lot of time off from your job in order to regain your stride. Because no career is more important than your own well-being and happiness, you'll want to make sure that you show yourself all the concern and compassion that you would show your best friend in a similar situation.

By addressing your health needs now instead of ignoring them until they are much more serious, you will be doing yourself the ultimate favor. If you need to lean on others at this point, make sure you do so. Sometimes asking for help is difficult for the independent person, but it might be absolutely necessary.

Entering Retirement

You've signed the papers, attended a celebration in your honor—and now, you could be at loose ends. Without any concrete career plans in mind, you might find yourself drifting from day to day like a ship with no one at the helm. You have choices in front of you, however—and depending on your age and energy level now, numerous possibilities still exist for you to find your ideal path of service.

If you decide to enter the workforce in some other capacity, you will quite readily transition into the Spring career season, with all its inherent potential for growth and change. On the other hand, should you choose to remain in retirement mode, you'll want to find other ways to fill your days—perhaps pursuing volunteer work, mentoring, or finding recreational activities that you've always wanted to try but never found the time for while you were working. Take a look at aarp.org for small business, legal, or medical information and much more.

GRETCHEN'S WINTER JOURNEY

A multifaceted woman whose greatest strengths are courage and persistence, Gretchen had experienced a rewarding career in the computer industry. Attaining an executive MBA with a focus on technology management, Gretchen was an expert in computer programming, and became a marketing manager in telecommunications for a large corporation. In the Summer of her career, Gretchen was at her peak in a field she enjoyed. Then catastrophe struck.

While working for a computer manufacturing company, Gretchen became very ill as a result of chemical poisoning. High levels of industrial chemicals causing violent illness were found in her body. Gretchen had become hypersensitive to any chemical she came in contact with, resulting in extreme physical reactions.

After being released from a hospital, Gretchen had to live in a bubble for two years.

Finding herself in the full force of the Winter career season, Gretchen could have given up—but she took steps to learn about her chemical sensitivity to bring about positive changes in her life.

Studying nutrition, detoxification, organic foods, natural allergy treatments, and environmental contaminates helped Gretchen to begin the painstaking path back to health. In the process, she received training in environmental assessment, and began her own company to assist people with personal environmental challenges. Now in the Spring of her career, Gretchen has a brand-new profession and a deep passion to help others on their path to wellness.

Gretchen has gained a new trust in her own heart's wisdom. As she says, "Intuition is a significant part of how I run my life." To this day, although she has recovered substantially from her chemical sensitivity, she utilizes her heart's wisdom on a regular basis.

Gretchen has an upbeat attitude and a clear sense of direction. She says, "Maintaining curiosity for life is important. People have the wherewithal to change careers and to make success happen for themselves." This Winter person successfully transitioned to a new season of growth.

You can do it too.

INNER CONTEMPLATION: THE MOUNTAINTOP

The Winter season can be like climbing a mountain—it may take a lot of energy and determination to get to the top. Once you reach the peak of the mountain, however, the hike down can seem like a breeze. Take stock of your own Winter challenges and how you've met them thus far. Have you reached the top of the mountain? Can you see a path on the other side of the summit heading toward Spring, with its opportunity for a new career start? If so, your own Spring may be just ahead.

Winter is a time of preparation coupled with a good dose of patience. Your energy level might be quite low now, and depending on your individual circumstances, you might be stretched to the breaking point or simply moving on to a new career cycle as part of a natural progression. The path out of your own Winter may demand all of the resources you can muster, but it will force you to take stock of where you've been and where you want to go from here.

Because the Winter season is an integral part of the career cycle, it happens to everyone at some time in their career lives. The key is in how you handle your own personal Winter.

MASTERING YOUR CAREER CYCLES

You are not here merely to make a living. You are here to enable the world to live more amply, with greater vision, and with a finer spirit of hope and achievement. You are here to enrich the world. You impoverish yourself if you forget this errand.

—WOODROW WILSON

TO BE IN COMMAND OF YOUR career cycles is to understand how they operate and how best to maneuver within their framework. By now you should have a solid grasp of your own career path and the methods needed to achieve professional success. Mastering the seasons of your career will take continued attention and effort. Your reward will be work that provides a service to others and provides the job fulfillment of your dreams.

LISTEN TO YOUR HEART'S WISDOM

There's a secret worth its weight in gold. It has to do with how to use your heart's wisdom in making employment and personal decisions. You may be offered a job that, on its face, appears to be the position of a lifetime, but something inside you says, "Don't take the job!" Do you listen to that wisdom, or do you ignore it and take a position that may end up to be your worst career nightmare? Ignoring your heart's wise words by jumping into a job that doesn't feel right is like putting away your umbrella when the Winter rain starts to fall—you may get drenched.

Heart's wisdom is a tool you can use to make the best choices for yourself. Your heart's wisdom circumvents the rational mind that requires proof by using the five senses. Your conscious mind prefers a safety net of hard facts, plans, and projections of the future. Unlike the logical mind, the heart doesn't need a safety net when it's up on the high wire. Working in tandem, the heart and mind can help you make a wise, educated career choice.

If you have an important career choice ahead of you, set your rational mind to work on it. Using that method, you'll likely collect an assortment of data that certainly can aid in the decision-making process. By also listening to your inner wisdom, you'll have that much more information to assist you in selecting the most advantageous alternative.

THE INNER GROWTH SPIRAL

Throughout your working life, you are given the opportunity to grow in both personal and professional ways. Career and personal growth can be likened to an upward spiral—where one continually develops more and more positive qualities and behaviors with the ultimate goal of reaching a point where actions enrich the self and others. A crowning achievement of climbing the upward spiral is to find your authentic path of service.

There is the potential to fall into a downward spiral as well, where one's behaviors become increasingly negative and end up detracting from the betterment of self and world.

You always have a choice as to which end of the spiral spectrum corresponds with your own values, beliefs, and goals. Do you desire to contribute your talents to the best of your ability in service to the world? Or do you wish to focus primarily on your own personal gain in any job you perform? The decision is yours alone.

There are many different levels of inner growth. Some people reach a higher level of spiritual maturity, with corresponding concern and generosity toward their fellow humans, while others remain entrenched in the egoistic and materialistic realms.

Be clear about where you fall in the spectrum of inner growth and what steps you may need to take to achieve a more advanced level of maturity. Remember the mirror on your career? Be clear about who you really are so that your image is an accurate one. If you're comfortable with your reflection in the mirror, you've mastered one of the most important steps of all. If you're not and you would like to modify your level of inner growth, you can do so simply by making the decision to change it.

INNER GROWTH AND CAREER SUCCESS

You can reach the top of your line of work and earn a large salary but still be on the low end of the inner-growth spiral. The act of attaining professional success does not mean that you will have made any advancement in personal growth whatsoever. If you achieve both career success and a high level of inner growth, chances are you will be on your path of service and fulfilled in your profession.

CLEANING OUT THE CLOSET

As a rule, you and your closest friends are at a similar level of inner development. We attract people of like minds into our lives as a natural, and not coincidental, occurrence. When you continually find yourself in circumstances where your friends and family are weighing you down instead of lifting you up, ask yourself why you're allowing that to happen. To be able to focus on the steps to your dream career, your relationships need to be peaceful and supportive, not troublesome or unhappy. Sometimes that may mean you will need to end, or withdraw from, relationships that aren't beneficial for you. Going through a process of removing the "dead weight" from your life (unwanted jobs or relationships) is like cleaning out a closet—in reality, you are making room for something better.

THE MORE YOU GIVE, THE MORE YOU GET

There is a career master law that says, "The positive energy you give to others ends up in your own hands. " Your generosity of spirit will reward you in many ways and will help to add more joy to the world. The pebble dropped into a pond creates enormous ripples, whether for positive or for negative. Which will you choose?

Holding on to your affection, time, money, or material possessions instead of sharing them is a miserly way to live. This doesn't mean that you need to scatter your money from a rooftop. Instead, be generous with your kind comments and helpful actions; these are things that don't cost you a cent. It takes no money out of your pocket to smile at someone—and it may brighten that person's day more than you realize. You will find that the more you open up your heart and give, the more comes back to you. But the key is to give because you care about others, not because there may be something in it for you later.

YOUR PATH OF SERVICE

Think of the best customer service you've ever received. Perhaps it was in a restaurant where the server was attentive without being cloying, competent without being obtrusive. He may have exemplified the ultimate in a food service professional, and you knew that you'd be back to that particular restaurant again because of that experience.

Your service to others during your career should be carried out with the same heartfelt dedication as the food server demonstrated. There is an ideal way to perform any job, whether it's in the janitorial field or the medical profession. The ultimate service in any career includes your whole being—your heart, mind, body, and soul.

If you find yourself in work that doesn't interest you enough to give it your all, then you're not in the right place.

There is a secret about work: if you love the job you have, you'll be able to leave it when the time is right. If you feel stuck in dreary or disagreeable work, it could be harder to extricate yourself from the situation.

There is every reason to look elsewhere if you are entrenched in a job that has passed its usefulness. So take action if you feel glimmers of job dissatisfaction. In the meantime, do the utmost to provide your personal best at your current job.

Various stumbling blocks can keep you from your path of service. Because these blocks are often disguised as elements of everyday life, you may not be aware of them at all—until you find yourself unable to reach your ideal career destination. Being aware of stumbling blocks is the key to transforming them into stepping-stones to success.

Fear

To be afraid is a part of the human condition. Learning how to control your fears is part of being a wise human!

The act of worrying is a form of fear—it wastes valuable mental energy. You have better things to do with your time than to work yourself into a frenzy about something that may never happen. Even if the thing you are worrying about does come to pass, all the anxious moments you spent thinking about it won't help.

Worry, fear, and anxiety are products of the conscious mind. They do not originate from your inner wisdom. Because they are indeed mental products, you have control over them to a large extent. You can send them on their way by using some of the techniques we introduced earlier.

To focus on faith that a situation will work out for the best, instead of on fear, which is the belief in a negative result, takes great mental command, but you can master your thoughts through patience and practice.

ERRONEOUS BELIEFS

Perhaps you've chosen not to pursue a certain career path because you're convinced that you lack the necessary ability to achieve it. Along the way you may have accepted as fact that you're not good enough even to try to reach your career dreams. Maybe people in positions of authority discouraged you by their doubtful comments, and you took on their beliefs as your own. It may be hard for you to entertain the idea of rekindling a career dream if you question your own abilities. Do you want to let others decide this for you?

The truth is that your path of service will be one that fits your skills, interests, and preferences flawlessly. When you've reached that ideal niche, it will feel just right. But first you will need to believe you can succeed.

This doesn't mean that you can become a high-paid runway fashion model at a height of four feet, seven inches, simply because you may desire it and believe you can achieve it. Your authentic path of service will match your physical attributes (if they have relevance to a particular job) as well as your skills.

A PERSON FOR ALL SEASONS

By consistently using the methods described in this book, you can transcend the cycle of career seasons. You'll become a person for *all* seasons, able to move flexibly through your career path.

There are several ways to traverse the seasons. You can go through them without much self-awareness and thus fail to see the many clues that could ease your path to a successful career. You might go through the seasons by listening to your heart's wisdom, and therefore have the inside scoop to propitious job moves that will save you time and energy. Ultimately, you may find your true path of service, which will allow you to integrate all career seasons in the best way.

In Figure 2, the four career seasons are represented as intersecting circles. As you can see, there are sections of commonality between each season, indicating areas of transition—where an individual leaves one season and enters the next. In a commonality zone, you might be exhibiting characteristics of, say, Spring, and begin to experience traits of the subsequent Summer season. There is no clear line of demarcation between one season and the next—there are always steps that lead up to, and out of, each career season.

The larger, outer square represents people who remain unaware of how best to handle their cycle of seasons. Unable to get to their path of service until they gain self-awareness, they stay on the outside looking in. In other words, they perpetuate an unfulfilling cycle of seasons.

If you've managed to make your way inside the smaller square, it means that you've discovered your authentic reflection in the career mirror.

✿ FIGURE 2 REFLECTIONS ON THE SEASONS

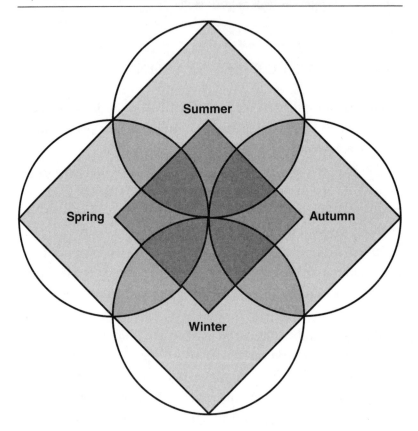

The center point (common radius) indicates your path of service. From this prime spot, you can draw from past seasonal experiences and notice promptly if you begin to stray from your authentic career path. You have an unobstructed view of all your career seasons at this point, which helps you to gain greater insight about your own job development and inner growth through the years.

IT'S UP TO YOU

Now, it's time to receive your diploma and go on your way—on a direct course to success. As you continue to travel through the cycle of seasons, keep in mind that there is something to be learned from every season, and that each has value and meaning in your life.

There is a place for you in the grand scheme of the universe. Your job is to follow your heart's wisdom to find that place, and then to use your own special talents to brighten the lives of others. Your responsibility is to listen carefully, act wisely, and hold up the lantern for others to follow.

ABOUT THE AUTHORS

KATHY SANBORN is a career expert, success consultant, and motivational speaker. She conducts a variety of career and personal-development workshops and holds private coaching sessions.

Kathy's articles on business and personal growth appear in many print and Internet publications. Her first book written with Wayne R. Ricci, *Grow Your Own Love*, teaches readers to increase the happiness in life through more satisfying relationships.

In her spare time, Kathy is a musician and songwriter. Her first smooth jazz album, *Critical Mass*, was released in 1996.

Wayne R. Ricci has broad experience in vocational counseling and personal and career coaching. Along with partner Kathy Sanborn, Wayne facilitates motivational and career development workshops geared to helping individuals achieve their professional dreams.

The duo's websites are lifeandcareercoaching.com and kathy sanborn.com.